SHARPEN YOUR TEAM'S SKILLS IN

*T*IME MANAGEMENT

SHARPEN YOUR TEAM'S SKILLS IN

*T*IME

MANAGEMENT

Jane Allan

The McGraw-Hill Companies

London · New York · St Louis · San Francisco · Auckland · Bogotá · Caracas
Lisbon · Madrid · Mexico · Milan · Montreal · New Delhi · Panama · Paris
San Juan · São Paulo · Singapore · Sydney · Tokyo · Toronto

Published by
McGraw-Hill Publishing Company
Shoppenhangers Road, Maidenhead, Berkshire, SL6 2QL, England
Telephone 01628 502500
Facsimile 01628 770224

British Library Cataloguing in Publication Data
Allan, Jane
  Sharpen your team's skills in time management
  1. Time management
  I. Title   II. Time management
  658.4'093

  ISBN 0 07 7092759

Library of Congress Cataloging-in-Publication Data
Allan, Jane
    Sharpen your team's skills in time management / Jane Allan.
      p.   cm. – (Sharpen your team's skills)
    Includes bibliographical references.
    ISBN 0-07-709275-9 (pbk. : alk. paper)
    1. Work groups–Time management.   I. Title.   II. Series.
  HD66.A47   1997
  658.5'421–dc20   96-46035
                                                      CIP

McGraw-Hill
A Division of The **McGraw·Hill** Companies

12345 CUP 9987

Typeset by BookEns Ltd, Royston, Herts
Printed and bound in Great Britain at the University Press, Cambridge

Printed on permanent paper in compliance with ISO Standard 9706

Contents

Series Preface   ix
About the Editorial Panel   xviii
About the Author   xv

1 Time management – an introduction   **1**
    Key learning points   1
    Introduction   1
    The 'Where does time go?' questionnaire   2
    Description of this book   13
2 Habit and attitude   **17**
    Key learning points   17
    Introduction   17
    Being too busy is a state of mind   18
    The part that habit plays   20
    How to manage your mind   22
    Summary   24
    Exercises   24
3 The time audit   **27**
    Key learning points   27
    Introduction   27
    Why audit time?   27
    The time audit sheets   29
    Tasks and task styles: their effect on the team 32
    What do we do now?   34
4 Prioritizing – the key to it all   **36**
    Key learning points   36
    Introduction   36
    Mission statements for all   37
    Analyse your tasks   40
    Take control over your life   43

	Summary	48
	Exercises and the learning contract	49
5	**Procrastination and can't say no**	**59**
	Key learning points	59
	Introduction	59
	The part procrastination plays in your life	60
	How to conquer fear	65
	Saying no constructively	71
	Summary	77
	Exercises	78
6	**Paper – its part in your downfall**	**88**
	Key learning points	88
	Introduction	88
	How to clear your desk and keep it clear	89
	A simple filing system works best	98
	Summary	102
	Exercises	102
7	**Communication**	**106**
	Key learning points	106
	Introduction	106
	How to write letters, memos and faxes that get read	107
	The quiet hour concept	113
	How to listen	116
	Summary	118
	Exercises	119
8	**Meetings – how to maximize their value**	**121**
	Key learning points	121
	Introduction	121
	How to organize the agenda	122
	The trick of note-taking	126
	How to take control in meetings	127
	Summary	131
	Exercises	132
9	**Drop-in visitors and delegation**	**141**
	Key learning points	141
	Introduction	141

The office layout – its part in your
  downfall   142
How to handle interruptions politely but
  firmly   147
How to delegate effectively   150
Summary   154
Exercises   155

Reading list   **160**
Index   **163**

SERIES PREFACE

This series of books focuses on sharpening the performance of your team by providing a range of training and support materials. These materials can be used in a variety of ways to improve the knowledge and skills of your team.

Creatiing high performance is achieved by paying attention to three key elements:

- The skills (competencies) of your people
- The way these skills are applied
- The support your people receive from you in applying their skills.

SKILL DEVELOPMENT

The books have been designed so that they can be used as individual workbooks.

The books in this series will provide materials for the development of a range of skills on a subject-by-subject basis. Each book will provide information and exercises in manageable chunks (lessons), which will be presented in a format which will allow you to choose the most appropriate way to deliver them to your staff. The contents will consist of all you need to guide your staff to a full understanding of the subject.

There are at least four ways you could choose to guide the learning of your team; these are:

- Training sessions
- Learning groups
- Open learning
- Experiential learning

TRAINING SESSIONS

These can be run by bringing your people together and guiding them step by step through the materials, including the exercises. During these sessions you can invite your people to interact with you and the materials by asking questions and relating the materials to their current work. The materials will provide you with the detailed information you need to present the subject to your team.

LEARNING GROUPS

This approach involves dividing your team into small groups (two, three or four people) and having a brief session with each group introducing them to the materials. Each group then works through the materials and meets with you from time to time to assess progress and receive your guidance.

OPEN LEARNING

This approach invites your people to use the materials at their own speed and in their own way. This is a form of individual learning that can be managed by regular meetings between you and your team as individuals or in a group. The process is started by introducing the materials to your team and agreeing some 'learning outcomes' to be achieved.

EXPERIENTIAL LEARNING

This calls for you to invite your team to examine the materials using the exercises as a focus, and then to get them to relate what they are learning directly to real-life situations in the workplace. This experience of learning is then shared and discussed by the team as a whole.

The books in the series have been designed to enable these four approaches to be used, as well as other ways that you might think are more appropriate to your team's specific needs.

APPLYING SKILLS

Time spent developing skills can be wasted if people do not have the opportunity to practise the skills. It is important that you consider this aspect of performance before embarking on a particular programme. It is useful to be able clearly to identify opportunities for practising skills and discussing these with your team. Providing opportunities for practising and further developing competency is part and parcel of the whole approach of this series.

PROVIDING SUPPORT

Once people have acquired a new skill and have been provided with opportunities to apply it, they still need your support and coaching while they are experimenting with using the skill. The opening book in this series, *Sharpen your skills in motivating people to perform*, provides clear guidance on how to help people to develop their skills and then how to provide experience, practice and support as they use their skills.

Before starting work with your team on the materials in this book, I suggest you do the following:

- Review the materials yourself
- Plan the approach you are going to follow
- Discuss what you are planning with your team
- Agree some learning outcomes
- Indicate how you are going to support your team during the learning process.

You can also make the materials relate to your specific circumstances by doing three things:

- Add local 'colour'
- Adjust the emphasis
- Integrate your own materials

The authors in the series have endeavoured to provide a range of materials that is comprehensive and will support you and your team. I hope that during this process you learn from and enjoy the experience.

Dr Trevor J. Bentley
Series Editor

ABOUT THE EDITORIAL PANEL

Dr Trevor Bentley, Series Editor for this series, is a freelance organizational consultant, a facilitator and a writer. Prior to becoming a consultant and while working as a senior executive, Trevor carried out a major research project into decision making and organization structures for which he was awarded his PhD. Over the last 20 years he has had a wide range of experience working with organizations in over 20 countries. Trevor has trained for four years with Gestalt South West and has attended Gestalt workshops in the UK and Europe. He now applies a Gestalt approach in his work.

Trevor has written 20 books and over 250 articles on business related issues. His background includes careers as a management accountant, financial director, computer systems designer, a management services manager, a human computer interface consultant, a trainer and a business manager. His current area of interest is in the application of a Gestalt approach to solving problems of organizational harmony. This includes culture change, performance management, team facilitation, executive coaching, mentoring and integrated supervision.

Susan Clayton is a leading contributor to the use and development of Gestalt philosophy and practice in organizations. Focusing on human processes, she enables managers and their staff to achieve business goals that depend on managing people. Her skill in raising awareness of how people relate to each other can forge supportive alliances and powerful co-operative relationships. Her approach includes helping people to manage blocks and difficulties in their contact with others, clearing the way for work and business relationships to move forward and grow.

Susan works with managers at all levels. Her interventions have aided groups in turmoil, managers needing to reach common agreement and individuals needing mentoring and coaching support. She helps organizations understand how to manage in a way that creates trust, respect and clarity in human relationships.

Mike Taylor is a consultant involved in the design, implementation and facilitation of personal and team development programmes within organizations. After graduating in 1987, he has worked with two outdoor management training providers, both as a manager and tutor. His work has a strong focus on the use of experiential learning in developing managers, mainly within larger organizations.

He also works with groups and single individuals in running meetings and events that help teams and individuals explore working practices and approaches. More recently he has developed an interest in Gestalt as a way of understanding group processes. He is a member of the Association for Management Education and Development.

Dr Tony Voss is a counsellor, consultant and trainer. He originally trained as a chemist before working in environmental research developing seagoing computer systems and information technology, and later in the computer industry as a project manager, consultant and quality manager. Tony has a particular interest in enabling people to contribute fully and creatively to their endeavours, and sees this as benefiting individuals, their organizations and society at large. He is an Accredited Counsellor with the British Association for Counselling, and he also trained in Gestalt over four years.

Tony works with those wanting to develop their organization and people, and those dealing with particular challenges in their working life. His clients also include those exploring the role of work in their life, as well as those with more personal issues.

*A*BOUT THE AUTHOR

Jane Allan is a Trainer. Qualified as a chartered accountant and a member of the Institute of Personnel Development, she had various careers as a bilingual secretary, a financial journalist, a training manager, a troubleshooter in an advertising agency and a partner in a firm of chartered accountants before she set up her own business in 1981.

Jane Allan & Associates is a training business providing training workshops in leadership, marketing, customer care, personal and financial awareness skills. Her time management workshop has been running since 1984 and it is from those many and varied presentations that she draws the tips for this book.

CHAPTER 1

TIME MANAGEMENT - AN INTRODUCTION

KEY LEARNING POINTS

- Where does time go?
- An overview of the art of managing time
- Learn to use habit rather than let it use you
- Learn how to manage your mind to let you change

INTRODUCTION

What does time mean to you? Are you like my mother of 86, watching the days go past ever slower, with time to stand and stare? Are you in a constant rush to get the best out of your day, always writing lists and never completing them? Is time money? Do you have time to stop and stare? What would you do if they extended every week by another day? If it were a working day? Or a weekend day? Do you even know what happens to time? Is it suddenly the end of the day and nothing done? Like Lewis Carroll's White Rabbit, does time fly for you?

What would you do if you knew exactly how long you had alive on this earth? How much of your life is planned? Nothing will ever happen in your life until you make time for it to happen. This book is about making time for things to happen: making time for work things to happen and making time for yourself too. The best way to start is as you intend to go along: by finding out what happens to your time and how to use it better. This introductory chapter will ask you some questions and at the end of the chapter it will give you some answers. These answers will lead you to read the various chapters in the book. The whole book can be used by a team to run its very own time management workshop over a time period chosen by that team. Some members of the team may prefer to use chapters individually, others may want to work in groups. Just use it, how you want to, when you want to and you will make time for things to happen in your life.

THE 'WHERE DOES TIME GO?' QUESTIONNAIRE

To complete the following questionnaire simply circle the letter that most nearly represents your views on how you behave in each of the situations described. If you feel you would never be in a particular situation, try to imagine how you might react if you were; not answering a question may adversely affect your final score.

When you have completed the questionnaire, score it using the form on page 6. Now take it in turns to compare your score with that of the rest of the team and plan how you will use this book to get the best out of the rest of your life.

TIME – WHERE DOES IT GO?

1. Time management is ...

    Doing one thing at a time, as planned A

    Working smarter not harder B

    Working effectively and leaving some things undone C

2. I am very busy but nothing seems to get done ...

    This is true A

    This is sometimes true B

    Not true, I get things done C

3. When I go away on holiday I ...

    Miss my job and call in a lot A

    Plan a full schedule and do lots B

    Laze around and enjoy the rest C

4. When I get home in the evening I ...

    Crash out, exhausted A

    Do something that's fun B

    Carry on working because I enjoy it C

5. I work at ...

    A rapid pace A

    A relaxed but steady pace B

    I don't work at all if I can help it C

6. If other people mess up the plans I made for the day I ...

    Get angry and feel guilty at not being productive A

    Use the time for thinking B

    Mutter a lot and blame them for my lack of productivity C

7. When I have to go away I ...

    Throw things into a bag at the last minute A

    Pack my bag well in advance B

    Make lists and pack my bag in good time C

8. When I was young and lived at home I was ...

    Free to run my own life as long as homework and chores got done A

    In full control of my own time B

    Told how to spend my time by my parents C

9. When I give a deadline I tend to finish the task ...

    Early A

    On time B

    Late or not at all C

10. I work best ...

    First thing in the day A

    After I have had some coffee B

    Last thing at night C

11. I use my best time to ...
      Get on with important tasks   A
      Plan my tasks   B
      Do whatever has to be done   C

12. I like best to ...
      Have many tasks on the go at once   A
      Get one thing done at a time   B
      Manage several tasks with staggered critical phases   C

13. Making a 'to do' list is ...
      Something I don't need to do   A
      What I always do   B
      Depressing because things never get done   C

14. Once I've made a 'to do' list I ...
      Stick to it and complete tasks in order   A
      Suffer from interruptions and lose the list   B
      Always get the whole list done   C

15. I sometimes work late or into the night because ...
      An urgent task has to be done   A
      I like the lack of interruptions   B
      I promised someone else the task would be done   C

16. It's quicker to ...
      Do it yourself   A
      Delegate it to someone else   B
      Involve the whole team   C

17. When travelling by train or plane I generally ...
      Use the time to relax   A
      Read something or find some work to do   B
      Not relevant, I always drive   C

18. If an unpleasant task is delegated to me, I ...
      Get it done first   A
      Work on it a bit at a time   B
      Put if off in the hope that it will go away   C

19. If I were self-employed I'd ...
      Have trouble setting priorities   A
      Have whole days doing nothing   B
      Be very productive   C

20. I never start anything until ...
      Someone puts pressure on me to get going   A
      I know the objectives and how I will tackle it   B
      I know I have time to complete it   C

21. If someone asks for my help with a task I usually ...
      Tell them I'm too busy   A
      Decline only when I know I haven't got the time   B
      Help them   C

22. The feeling that maybe I've taken on too much . . .
    Is always with me   A
    Comes to me from time to time   B
    Is one I never feel   C
23. Around here there is a last-minute rush . . .
    Always   A
    Only when the unexpected occurs   B
    Never, we work calmly at times   C
24. When there is a crisis I . . .
    Panic and rush around a lot   A
    Delegate it to someone outside the organization   B
    Go sick   C
25. If other people are late for appointments I . . .
    Always get very annoyed   A
    Understand that they are doing their best   B
    Treat it as an opportunity to get on with something   C
26. Delegation means . . .
    More time to explain than to do it yourself   A
    An opportunity to help others grow   B
    The only way to get everything done   C
27. When I attend meetings I am . . .
    Always on time   A
    Always late   B
    Optimistic about how long they will take   C
28. My desk is . . .
    Clear at night   A
    Clear apart from what I'm working on   B
    Buried under a heap of paper, files and clutter   C
29. If I'm looking for something I . . .
    Can put my hand on it straightaway   A
    Can never find it when I need it   B
    Don't understand our filing system   C
30. When it comes to passing on information I . . .
    Send an E-mail   A
    Call every person I need to speak to and chat   B
    Never need to   C

THE SCORING SHEET

Question number	A	B	C	Total
1	0	4	2	
2	0	2	4	
3	4	0	2	
4	0	2	4	
5	4	2	0	
6	4	2	0	
7	0	4	2	
8	2	4	0	
9	4	2	0	
10	4	2	0	
11	2	4	0	
12	4	0	2	
13	4	2	0	
14	4	0	2	
15	0	2	4	
16	0	4	2	
17	2	4	0	
18	4	2	0	
19	4	2	0	
20	0	4	2	
21	4	0	2	
22	0	2	4	
23	0	4	2	
24	0	2	4	
25	0	4	2	
26	0	4	2	
27	2	0	4	
28	2	0	4	
29	2	4	0	
30	2	4	0	
GRAND TOTAL SCORE				

INTERPRETING THE SCORE

RANGE **INTERPRETATION**

0–39 **You are a slave to time.**

Time worries you and yet you have no idea of how to manage it. You generally deliver too little too late. Your life is disorganized, people find you unreliable and you let them down. You are usually working in crisis and alternating between rushing to get things done and sinking back into an exhausted state. You need to relax and use this book to help you plan your time with care.

40–65 **You are balanced in your approach to time.**

You are neither a slave nor a master of time. You usually get the work done and are neither rushed nor pressurized by your job. Other people in the team are more productive than you but you don't let this worry you. For you, enjoying life counts far more than getting the job done. You need to use this book to help you put the best into your work without affecting your life.

66–89 **You are a master of time.**

Did you write this book? Maybe you could have done. You have mastered time. You are well organized and get things done without becoming a victim of your own efficiency. You understand prioritizing and practise it. Lots of things happen in your life because you have allowed the time to let them happen. Although you are very good at time management there may be some tips in this book that can help you further. Use your own abilities to help the rest of the team learn.

90–120 **You are obsessed with time.**

The management of time is an obsession with you. You drive yourself too hard and often bite off more than you can chew. Probably you are a workaholic. Certainly you need to learn to say no, to relax and recharge your batteries. This book is for you: every chapter will show you how to extend your life and yet achieve more.

EXPLANATION OF QUESTIONS

1. **TIME MANAGEMENT IS ...**
   Good time management is not about working harder, it is not about filling every day to the utmost and collapsing exhausted at night. It is about working smarter. It may mean leaving something undone but only the unimportant, not the 'don't want to' tasks.

2. **I AM VERY BUSY BUT NOTHING SEEMS TO GET DONE ...**
   Being too busy is a state of mind, being at a loose end is to be undisciplined. Good time management means that you will normally have time to accomplish all you set out to but sometimes there will be extra busy times; these will mean you have to plan for the unplanned in the form of a crisis plan.

3. **WHEN I GO AWAY ON HOLIDAY I ...**
   You can love your job but it is good to love life too. Probably the best thing to do with a holiday is to relax. Most people achieve more in 28 weeks of the year than they could ever do in 52 year after year. If you can plan your holiday to relax for part of the time and explore for the rest you will have fresh intellectual stimulation. By the way, you need a holiday – notice this question assumes you take one!

4. **WHEN I GET HOME IN THE EVENING I ...**
   If you carry on working you will not work well or achieve more, all you'll do is work longer. Take work home only on an exceptional basis and then make sure that you compensate yourself well at other times. If you crash out when you get home you are either working too hard at work or too lazy to make the most of your own life. Get an interest, take up sport or a hobby – but do something for your own sake to make the most of your life.

5. **I WORK AT ...**
   If you rush at everything you will make mistakes and feel exhausted. Take your time and plan your day; you will get more done and not feel so hassled.

6. IF OTHER PEOPLE MESS UP THE PLANS I MADE FOR THE DAY I ...

If you take work with you to meetings or appointments you will always have something to do if you are kept waiting. They are making you a gift of extra time that day.

7. WHEN I HAVE TO GO AWAY I ...

Planning time helps make sure that you forget nothing. It is a good idea to keep lists if you travel a lot so that you can make sure you never forget the key items. Another good idea is to pack your bag or even your briefcase the night before so that there are no added pressures in the morning.

8. WHEN I WAS YOUNG AND LIVED AT HOME I WAS ...

Time management is a discipline that you begin to learn during your adolescent years. If your parents took too much control over your life, you will find it hard to manage time now.

9. WHEN I GIVE A DEADLINE I TEND TO FINISH THE TASK ...

While it is good to get a task out of the way and finish early, time deadlines are budgets to guide you, not targets to exceed. Don't turn your time management into a race against the clock to prove yourself. Even when you underpromise and overdeliver to a customer or client you still have a budget for time which is accurate and a target which you give the customer. It is the target you seek to overdeliver in order to delight the customer but in truth you will have come in on budget.

10. I WORK BEST ...

Very few people are really at their best at the end of the day. The fresher you are the more likely you are to be productive.

11. I USE MY BEST TIME TO ...

You are a fool to yourself if you do not plan your best time. Use it to get on with important tasks, not just any old task.

12. I LIKE BEST TO ...

Answers A and C are the best project management practices. There is danger, though, in too much variety: you may find it hard to settle to one task with so many others calling on your time.

13. MAKING A 'TO DO' LIST IS . . .

Really good management of time means taking stock regularly of the tasks that are waiting to be done. And this is something to do every day, probably at the start of the day or last thing the night before. Take the opportunity to review and revise the priorities on the list.

14. ONCE I HAVE MADE A 'TO DO' LIST I . . .

If your 'to do' list is a good one with priorities listed you should be able to negotiate as temptations occur and as a result get a lot, sometimes even all, of your tasks done systematically in order of priority. You will not be able to stick to it rigidly at all times – not if you work in the real world, that is. You will have to be flexible and change priorities to meet changing circumstances.

15. I SOMETIMES WORK LATE OR INTO THE NIGHT BECAUSE . . .

Sometimes we all have to work late for reasons outside our own control but it should not become habit-forming. If you work late to avoid interruptions you need to establish a quiet hour; Chapter 7 on communication will tell you how to do just that.

16. IT IS QUICKER TO . . .

The joy of teams is that they combine diverse people in one work group. The very diversity of the team means that it is usually quicker to work as a team than to work alone. It is never quicker to do everything yourself but those who hate to delegate always believe so. Nor is it a good idea to dump all problems on someone else, although in a crisis that might be the best way forward.

17. WHEN TRAVELLING BY TRAIN OR PLANE I GENERALLY . . .

Put the time to the best use for you. Driving yourself everywhere you go takes up your energy and may not be the best use of your time. Relaxing, or possibly catching up with your reading pile, may be the right thing to do.

18. IF AN UNPLEASANT TASK IS DELEGATED TO ME, I . . .

Do it first and get it over with is usually the best. The more time you spend putting a task off the longer it hangs around to annoy you and oppress you. Very often these tasks once tackled are not as bad as they seemed in the in-tray.

19. IF I WERE SELF-EMPLOYED I'D ...

Self-employed people have to regulate their own lives, they have to self-motivate. It is sometimes better to plan for whole days doing nothing so that the brain can relax and have an opportunity to think. If you plan all the time you have, you never have enough time. Not getting started at all is something quite different and not to be proud of. Chapter 5 on procrastination needs to be carefully read by all budding entrepreneurs.

20. I NEVER START ANYTHING UNTIL ...

There are two rules to taking on a task: make sure you have time to complete it and make sure you know the objectives and have allocated time to plan how they will be achieved. Never wait for others to get you going, get going by yourself.

21. IF SOMEONE ASKS FOR MY HELP WITH A TASK I USUALLY ...

Nice people get taken for granted but you don't have to be nasty to get things done. Help when you can but only if you really have the time. There are a lot of abdicators in this world and you may have subordinates or team members who like to delegate upwards.

22. THE FEELING THAT MAYBE I'VE TAKEN ON TOO MUCH ...

We all take on too much at times but if that is a constant emotion there is something wrong. Learn to say no with the help of Chapter 5. Not taking on enough is not fulfilling your real potential so don't fall into that trap either.

23. AROUND HERE THERE IS A LAST-MINUTE RUSH ...

Some organizations make it harder for their staff to be efficient. Perhaps it feels exciting, perhaps it seems to engender a good atmosphere, but nothing really gets done and fully completed. Every team, every organization should plan to accomplish its normal workload in such a way that there is spare time for genuine crises and the unexpected opportunities that may arise.

24. WHEN THERE IS A CRISIS I ...

Pressure hits us in many ways: some overreact with extra energy which is wasteful, others withdraw from the situation. Good crisis management is simple – it is the art of being prepared for the unknown and delegating outwards.

25. IF OTHER PEOPLE ARE LATE FOR APPOINTMENTS I . . .

You always have other work you can do, get on and do it. Don't waste time making blame or getting annoyed; treat the time instead as a bonus factor.

26. DELEGATION MEANS . . .

The world is too complex, tasks too many for one person to be able to do everything except in the smallest of businesses and even there it is good to have someone to talk things over with. Time teamwork is what gets things done.

27. WHEN I ATTEND MEETINGS I AM . . .

Being on time is polite, efficient and the sign of a good time manager. Being late is rude and takes no account of a social contract that exists. Other people may have planned their time and if you are late you are showing total disregard for them.

28. MY DESK IS . . .

Each day is the first day of the rest of your life, do you really want to begin it with the detritus of yesterday? A clear desk at night is essential for security and fire precautions, but a mucky desk in the day is just a hindrance.

29. IF I'M LOOKING FOR SOMETHING . . .

Most filing systems work against the users and for storage. Make sure any system you have makes retrieval its key. Never rely on your memory – it may fade one day and it certainly won't be there when you are not!

30. WHEN IT COMES TO PASSING ON INFORMATION . . .

Sending an E-mail is probably the most time efficient option, provided that you do not resort to E-mails when a face-to-face encounter is what is needed. Everyone has something to tell others; poor communication is what destroys organizations.

Now read through the following description of the rest of this book so that you can decide which of the chapters is the one to tackle first. Of course the book has been written in a systematic order so you may well prefer to start with Chapter 2 and work on to the end. It is up to you; use it to the best of the team's advantage – and have fun!

DESCRIPTION OF THIS BOOK

We all know what it is like to reach the end of a day and feel that we have achieved nothing. Hours have passed in apparently fruitless activity and yet we were there and hardly seemed to have time to draw breath. No one is immune from this disease but thank goodness it is treatable. Work your team through this guide and you will have treated both the symptoms and the root cause of all the team's suffering (and yours too).

To begin, everyone needs to understand habit. Habits are good things, they save us time and brain energy, but sometimes they build habit paths that trigger instant reactions that are no longer relevant to the situation. In working through this guide you will start in Chapter 2 by examining the team's habits. Do they help? Or do they hinder? For example, knowing your route to work so well that you don't have to read a map each day certainly saves you time and anxiety. It frees up your brain to concentrate on the traffic and other road users. At least I trust that is what you do!

But have any members of your team got into any bad habits? Do you leap to any conclusions because things have always happened in a certain way? Does anyone ever start a routine task without asking if this is the day when it changes? Because there *is* a day when it changes and if you miss that day your habit starts to become a hindrance in the pursuit of good time management. Many years ago I worked as an auditor in a firm of accountants; our job was to audit our clients and to report to the shareholders, we had standard files and guidance notes to help us. But every now and then there was a different situation, a need for another type of report, a client that was not subject to audit. The temptation to take the usual pack of material out to the client and browbeat it through was very great. We had to stop and think. If we didn't stop and think the costs on the work would rise sky-high and we would not get paid.

So the solution is to conduct a time audit. Now conducting a time audit is very boring. It means you must all stop at regular intervals during the day and write down exactly and honestly what you are doing – even if what you are doing is not what the boss might want you to be doing. It has to be a very personal document, one in which there is no vested interest to lie or to fool yourself. And yet the paradox is that if a whole team were to conduct a time audit together over the same period of time, those time audits would be even more valuable because they would show the knock-on effect of time consumption. Chapter 3 is an exercise in time auditing – be brave, tackle the project as a whole team but feel free to keep some of the notes you make to yourselves.

Now you know what you do and you understand why you do it: all that remains is to cure yourself of the less helpful habits and install some good ones. This is of course the hardest part of the exercise. Easy to write, easy to say but very hard to carry through day after day. But help and hope come in the guise of the team: together you will learn how to use the strengths of those around you to reinforce your new behaviours.

The key to it all is setting and keeping to an effective list of priorities. To do this everyone needs to know the goals of the department, the division and of the organization as a whole. Those organizations that have set mission statements and philosophies of operation are helping their people to prioritize and as a result help themselves to achieve. But what do you do if your organization has not written a mission statement or, even worse, if the mission statement seems to have nothing to do with the work for which you are responsible? Relax, Chapter 4 has thought of that. Every organization large or small can relate to the simple mission statement available for you to adapt. And anyway you can do better than that: you know why you are here and what value your job adds to the whole – brainstorm it together as a team and you'll have the mission statement you need.

The problem comes when your list of priorities does not match that of your boss, subordinates or worse still the dragon from another department. It happens to us all. Which is why like any set of objectives, the priorities you set need to be SMART – Specific, Measurable, Achievable, Realistic and Timely – but unlike most other objectives they need to be flexible, too. Never fill your day completely with planned events: something will always happen to throw the plan. I was taught this many years ago by a teacher at school who finished with the words, 'If you end up with some spare time, you can always use it to dream or make a million'. Each team member's aim is to get the time to make a million, even if only in their dreams.

Before I sat down to write this chapter I thought, 'I'll just get this out of the way, then my desk will be clear'. Funny how one 'just' can lead to another and a whole day can pass by without the major task being tackled at all. Procrastination catches us all. Any team member who has a piece of paper in his or her in-tray with a coffee stain on it and a curly corner, has something over which she or he has procrastinated. Why? Don't know how to start? Don't want to start? What are you afraid of? In Chapter 5 I'll show you how to show your team to side-step procrastination once and for all.

Possibly the worst enemy of time is the fear of saying 'no'. Sometimes we have to say no to bosses, colleagues, subordinates, friends and even clients or customers. No one finds it easy but those who can do it get their time back and a chance to plan it for themselves. By rejecting a task you do not reject a person. We all feel guilty if we say no to a request but it is not the same as wishing that person were dead or condemning them to hell. We are simply indicating how that person's request fits into our overall priorities. Worried? Don't be, Chapter 5 will show you and your team ways to say no that are polite, constructive and get your message across without offending anyone or bringing the wrath of hell down about your ears.

'I know I've got it, I saw it just a few moments ago.' This statement is made while hurriedly 'scrubbling' through piles of paper scattered all over a desk. And the trouble is, the relevant piece never comes to light in time. Does any team member have to call people back 'when they've found it'? Can everyone put a hand on everything they might need within 60 seconds? Or do people stick Post-it™ notes on chairs because the desk is too full? The trouble is that most people do not understand the art of filing. Chapter 6 will show you how to control the paper that lands on desks in a way that gives you repeated and effective access to it. Chapter 6 will also help out others who suffer from your team's paper distribution network!

Which members of your team love answerphones? If they do, it is because every message they leave has been pre-planned and they know exactly what to say. Most of us, telephone sales people aside, do not prepare a script before making a phone call and yet it can save so much time and ensures that your message gets across as effectively as possible. Chapter 7 will give you tips and ideas on how to make sure the members of your team plan all communication so as to save their time, your time and that of your correspondents. Leave it open on your desk to help the worst offenders in other teams that you have to deal with!

'He's in a meeting – still it beats working, doesn't it?' I overheard that remark in the office of one of my clients. It was made by an exasperated secretary who had been trying to make contact with someone all day long. When the man concerned completed his time audit he found that in one week he had spent over three days in meetings, leaving just two days for him to do his job – and it was not a part-time job, it involved running a factory making precision products. Of course meetings are essential; run well they save time but run badly they are the most expensive waste of time I know. Have you ever sat in a meeting listening to colleagues talking about something that does not interest or involve you, thinking about all the things you could be doing, only to wake up when they mention your name because they have moved on but you didn't notice? Yes?

Chapter 8 is for you. In it you will find tips on controlling agendas, organizing start and finish times and generally making the meeting cost-effective.

So far we have not looked at the effect other people can have on the team's management. If anyone finds that every time he or she settles down to a really tricky task someone smiles and says 'Have you got a minute?', then that team member suffers from drop-in visitors. They mean well, they are stuck and need your help, they want to chat, they even have something you want but not right now! But we are back to the problem of being nice, and of course it is quicker to say 'What is it?' than to put them off, or so you might think. You can't cure them all, not unless you get the whole organization you work for to let you train every team to work to its ideas and suggestions – but you can control other teams with gentle humour and a helpful solution to any root causes; Chapter 9 tells you how to help the team control interruptions.

Of course some of those drop-in visitors are a result of poor delegation or lack of delegation. Some too may be trying for a bit of upward delegation. And the trouble with delegation is that it is quicker and safer to do it yourself – or so some people think. If any one team member's in-tray is full and others are chatting, if some team members never see the bottom of the pile because there is always something added, if anyone feels overworked, maybe team delegation is the answer. Good delegation can take as much as five times the amount of time it would take to do the task yourself; so how can it be part of good time management? Because good delegation means that you may never have to do the task again and if you couple it with empowerment it means that team members may even find ways independently to help each other. In Chapter 9 you'll discover some really good delegation ideas.

Working through this first chapter will tell you where the time management problems lie. Use the 'Where Does Time Go?' questionnaire to decide which of the remaining chapters are the most crucial to work through. Don't feel that you have to work through them in the order in which they appear in the book. Deal with the most important and obvious time problems for your team first. Each of the chapters will give you good tips on key topics. Work through them together with your team and draw on the energy of the whole team to maximize your time performance together.

CHAPTER 2

HABIT AND ATTITUDE

KEY LEARNING POINTS

- Being too busy is a state of mind
- Discover the part that habit plays in your life
- Learn to use habit rather than let it use you
- Learn how to manage your mind to let you change

INTRODUCTION

This chapter shows you and your team how to get the best from yourselves by controlling habit and making it work for you. It also invites you to be honest in looking at your attitude to time and time management.

First, we look at the way people perceive time and its management. So much has been written and said on the subject that it is almost impossible for anyone not to have a view. Dependent on the ingrained nature of the view, including the 'It's quicker to do it myself' approach, is your ability to manage time. Positive mental set goes a long way here.

The next part of the chapter explains the uses and drawbacks of habit paths. The exercises help each member of your team to examine the habit paths they use and check their continued validity. What was a good habit a year or even a month ago could be a bad one today. As long as habit is working for you it constitutes a short cut and a possible time-saver, but when it works against you it is a hurdle over which you have to leap before you are able to manage time.

The section on managing your mind will help team members to understand their approach to the way they work. It includes a simple introduction to **transactional analysis** (TA) and shows individuals how to use TA to understand themselves better. You may find that you prefer to allow your team to use this section of the chapter individually, although it can be fun to work together.

Finally, there are a number of exercises at the end of the chapter. You can use them as learning tools with the team or set them for individual team members to tackle alone to ensure that they have absorbed the key learning points of the chapter.

BEING TOO BUSY IS A STATE OF MIND

I have run seminars on the subject of time management for over 20 years. Until the recession of the 1990s, which brought the dramatic downsizing and apparent rightsizing policies into organizations, I always took the view that it was rare to find someone who genuinely had too much to do. After all, work expands to fill the desks available and looking busy was an art we all cultivated. That is not true today. I don't believe it will ever be true again. But I do believe that outside start-up situations it continues to be rare to find someone who *constantly* has too much to do. Most people suffer from periods of heavy workload: for accountants it will be month- and year-end periods, for sales people it will fall at the peak seasonal times for the business, while for each of us sickness, holidays and new projects will always add their burden of work pressure.

If you genuinely fall into the category of consistently, day-in day-out, having too much to do, you must consider the following:

- *Are you failing to delegate*   See Chapter 9 for some practical help.
- *Are you a perfectionist who has gone beyond the bounds of quality into the realm of overload?*   Take a deep breath and re-address your priorities with the help of Chapter 4.
- *Is your job really too big for one person?*   In which case you must talk this through with your boss and establish personal objectives.
- *Do you waste time for part of the day and then panic during what is left because you genuinely do have too much to do in the remaining time?*   See Chapters 4 and 5 for some practical help.
- *Have you been a victim of upward delegation? Or even of a downward dump?*   Turn to Chapter 5 for help in saying no.
- *Or do you suffer from an attitude of mind?*

Many years ago, when I was still at school, I cultivated an image of being busy, overworked, under pressure and too busy to deal with unimportant things. I was rapidly brought down to reality by a teacher who told me that the absent-minded professor was dead and that if I wanted to get on in the world I would need to make sure everything I did led to where I wanted to be. In other words, I needed to rethink my attitude.

Perhaps we ought to quote Henry Ford here: 'Whether you think you can, or whether you think you can't, you're right.' In other words, it is attitude of mind that is the key. At this stage I am sure a number of people reading this chapter will be revisiting their own inbuilt attitudes and saying to themselves something like, 'that's all very well, but ...'.

Like me, you probably never seem to have enough time and yet we have all the time there is. My mother is over 80 and finds the opposite problem: days are too long for her to fill them as she used to. Where is the device that allows her to sell to you and me part of the time she has going spare, so that she could supplement her meagre pension income?! Without such a device we have to do this for ourselves. The problem is not, and cannot be, a shortage of time but rather what you and I do with the time we have got. So any effort on attitude must begin with stopping and starting. We must stop thinking:

- I'm too busy
- There isn't enough time
- How am I going to cope?
- I'm bad at time
- I can't do that in the time

and start thinking:

- I can achieve that
- There's plenty of time
- This is my coping plan
- I manage my time well
- I can do it.

Perhaps a Chinese proverb may help too: 'Besides the noble art of getting things done, there is the noble art of leaving things undone. The wisdom of life lies in eliminating the non-essentials.'

Of course you cannot change your attitude overnight, it will take time, but you can start right now, this minute, as you read this chapter – really, you can. Here is how to do it. Take a sheet of paper and write on it all your thoughts, beliefs and ideas about time and time management. Write down what you believe to be true. This does not have to be in great detail, but the more you think about how you feel about time, the more you will have a clear picture of the way your mind is working and the easier it will be to change the attitude of your mind. Once you have completed your sheet of paper, go through all the thoughts you have written down and mark the negative ones, the ones you want to stop having. Now take another sheet of paper and re-write each of the negative thoughts as a positive one. Turn round your thinking and attitude in this way and read the sheet regularly until you get to the point where if you wrote down your attitude of mind again it would contain all the positive thoughts and none of the negative ones. But please don't become smug. You are setting your-self a good attitude for the time – and times change. In due course you will need to review and revise your attitude again. Remember the paradox of change? The only constant is change itself.

THE PART THAT HABIT PLAYS

Habits are the key to success. Habits that work for you are good habits, and good habits are the mental programming that successful people use to keep themselves ahead of the pack. Indeed you might like to think about the concept that successful people not only form good habits, they form the habit of doing things others have not thought of or are not prepared to do.

First, you need to check out your habit paths. What are the things that you do automatically at work without thinking, and are these always good things to have done? Make a list of your habits. You will not find this easy. The best way to tackle it is to keep a daily log of what you do and the time at which you do it, noting also whether you always do something in a particular way. Keep the log for at least a week and preferably for longer; at the end of it you will be able to spot your habits at a glance. Go through the log with a marker pen and highlight the repetitive habit approaches you find. Mark the same habit in the same colour. Now make a list of the habits you have found: are they always good? If the answer is yes, keep the habit, but if the answer is no and:

- this leads me to react rather than act
- this is really a bad habit
- this makes it harder for me to get what I want
- this costs me time
- this costs other people time
- I do this for all the wrong reasons
- I don't know why I do this
- a leopard cannot change his spots

you will need to change the habit. Change is easy, it happens around us all the time. You and I are humans, we are proactive, we can change whenever we want to. That is the problem in a nutshell: we can change when we want to but to change we have to want to change. Perhaps you like your habits, bad though they may be. Because they are habits they will resist change with all the force of a child that goes rigid because it does not want to do something its parent is encouraging it to do. A later section of this chapter will show you how to manage your mind.

THE HABIT CHANGE PLAN

1. *Identify the habits (one at a time) that you wish to change.* Your daily habit log will tell you what to do.
2. *Set your attitude to positive.* Tell yourself that changing this habit is possible and you will achieve it.
3. *Define the replacement habit you wish to adopt.* Take care to record the proposed new habit in great detail so that you can fall back on your plan for help. Remember, your attitude log may help you here.
4. *Develop a realistic action plan to introduce the new habit.* For example, imagine that you have decided to form the habit of learning people's names. Set yourself a target that is realistic and achievable yet will give you the stretch you need to make challenge part of the equation. Do not say 'I'll learn the name of everyone I meet this week'. Say instead 'I'll learn the name of one new person per day this week'. The second intent is achievable, yet challenging. The first option is too open-ended and may not be possible if you attend a large gathering of people.
5. *Start to behave according to the habit you wish to adopt.* Since you will have to encourage yourself, work out little rewards to build into your new routine. Put up signs all round your work space to remind you of the new habit path and let these reinforce the behaviour. Watch out for the old triggers that made the habit what it was. For example, if you plan to change the habit of smoking, and used to light a cigarette every time you spoke on the phone, watch out for the trigger of the phone ringing to jump-start you back into the old habit. Put a sign right by the phone and move any smoking paraphernalia away from the phone area. Make it easy for yourself.
6. *Stick firmly to your new behaviour pattern until it has become a habit.* You will at some stage be tempted with the thought 'Just this once won't matter' – it will. Any deviation from the new norm to the old habit will simply reconfirm the old habit path.
7. *Get help with your planned habit change.* It used to be called

nagging, now it is help – help to change a habit. Tell everyone what you are doing and they will soon remind you when you don't do it. Alternatively pick one, two or three reliable people to help you change that habit. Brief them fully and give them your permission to nag you should you show signs of weakening in your resolve. But do remember not to bite their heads off if they do nag you; they are only trying to help.

8. *Start.*   This is the most important point of all – most of us are capable of talking about what we intend to do without doing anything at all. Make sure you talk about it *and* do it.

When it comes to choosing a new habit, you must remember that by choosing a habit you choose the results of that habit. So you must think about the likely outcome before setting off on a new habit path. Sometimes one habit leads across another habit path and has the effect of changing more than one outcome at once: think all this through before selecting the new habit.

HOW TO MANAGE YOUR MIND

Throughout this chapter we have been thinking and talking about change: change in the way we do things and change in attitude. Because we are creatures of habit, change isn't always comfortable. It can make us feel nervous, even afraid, of unknowns and altered outcomes. But we must accept that the only constant in this world is change. First, we must realize that fear of the unknown is just that, fear of something we do not know and once we know it it will be unlikely to hold any fears for us.

The first elements of key knowledge you need are about yourself or, I could say, what makes you tick: why you react to certain situations in the way you do and not in the way others do. If you understand yourself you can control your reactions and you can use your self-knowledge to bring about the changes you need.

Begin by thinking about your reactions to other people. Imagine that you have delegated a piece of work to someone else, someone who is very reliable most of the time but not all of the time. Imagine too that you were very busy today and did not check what that individual has done. Now picture yourself with your own boss or someone else important and imagine that you pick up the piece of work and start to go through it with this third party. As you go through it the other person draws your attentions to a mistake. It is a big one and it is waving at you, straight off the page. What will you say?

- 'Forgive me, I need to come back to you on this one, there seems to be a bit of a problem.' (A)
- 'Oh no, the computer has played up again, it's so unreliable.' (B)

Now those may not be your exact words but I think you can see the gist of what you might say. In the first instance, (A), you deliver no blame and react totally calmly; in the second instance, (B), you deliver blame maybe to another person, perhaps outside the organization but probably onto an inanimate object that cannot defend itself.

Now let's get back face to face with the very person who made the mistake. Remember, this person is usually quite reliable but I have painted a picture in which your failure to check his or her work has probably compounded your fury. What are you going to say to this person?

- 'Thanks a bunch, you really dropped me in it. Why didn't you do what I told you to do?' (C)
- 'There seems to be a problem here somewhere, let's have a look at it together.' (D)

Again you might not choose these exact words but the gist of them would be in the first instance, (C), to issue blame in some way and to give the implication that you would have done better. The second set of words, (D), is very similar to (A) above: it allocates no blame and represents a totally calm reaction. Which are your two chosen reactions, one to each of the sketched situations? Please think about what your reaction would be on a bad day, not a good one; would it change in any way?

In the terminology of **transactional analysis** (TA) your reactions are either Parent, Adult or Child – Parent if you criticize or imply that you know better, Adult if you stay calm and unemotional at all times and Child if you try to push the blame on someone else. Each of us is a mix of all three of these reactions, which are known as **ego states**. The reactions given above can be defined as follows:

- A is the Adult reaction
- B is the Child reaction
- C is the Parent reaction
- D is the Adult reaction.

For the purpose of this understanding no one reaction is any better or any worse than the others; each is merely information, information about how you react in different circumstances.

SUMMARY

We are proactive not reactive. Habits may be formed in early life and later as a result of our working experiences, but those habits can be changed – if we want to change them, that is. The first step towards change is to realize that you have habits that do not work in your favour. Next, you need to decide which habits you should change and how to go about it. There is no doubt that each of us can change if we put all of our energy into making that change happen. It is possible to think positive and make positive happen. Just as pessimists are never disappointed, optimists will always see the opportunity and run with the challenge.

EXERCISES

Exercise 2.1 – Attitude survey

You will need:

- flipcharts
- coloured flipchart pens
- time: about 30–45 minutes.

Now write a series of statements that are bound to get a reaction from your team. The statements should be work-oriented and time-orientated. For example:

For an accounts team:

The budget tax has to be completed one month early this year

For a human resource team

Appraisals will be conducted one month early this year

Ask your team members to write down their attitudes to these generic statements and then discuss the attitudes in the group. How can we make them more positive? What is the normal initial reaction and what relationship does it bear to the normal final reaction?

Exercise 2.2 – Habit track

Ask team members to make a note of any habits they believe they have, dividing the habits between helpful and hindering ones. Team members will then bring their habit lists to the meeting.
You will need:

■ flipcharts (one per group of three or four)
■ coloured flipchart pens
■ time: about half an hour.

Each team member will prepare a piece of paper listing his or her most significant good habit. Pass each piece of paper around the group and ask each team member to tick (✓) the habits they feel are good and cross (X) the habits they feel are bad.

Choose one good habit from each team member that is seen by the majority of the team to be a good habit, and discuss how this habit can be enhanced. Then, choose one habit that is seen by the individual to be a good habit but is not seen as such by team members. Why? What should the team member do?

Exercise 2.3 – Building new habit paths

The purpose of this exercise is to help team members build new habits. It must be done after all the other exercises and can be used as a summary session.
You will need:

■ flipcharts
■ coloured flipchart pens
■ a scarf to be used as a blindfold.

Ask team members to fold their arms. Look carefully at the way they fold their arms and ask all those who fold them with the left arm uppermost to remain in position. Now ask those who fold their arms with the right arm uppermost to copy those who fold their arms the opposite way. Team members will have difficulty in folding their arms in the unusual way. Ask those who normally fold their arms with the left arm uppermost to teach the others how to fold their arms in this way.

Next, ask the right-arm uppermost team members to train the left-arm uppermost team members to fold their arms in the opposite way. Each group will have broken a habit path and opened up to new opportunities.

Now ask for a volunteer. Ask that person to be ready to

conduct an experiment first with eyes open and then blindfolded. Other team members should stand around the room in order to create people-barriers. Then ask the volunteer to walk past and around the barriers without touching anyone. Have that person do the walk several times. Now ask him or her to do the walk again, blindfolded this time. Team members must *not* move.

Next, allow two members of the people-barriers to move and ask the blindfold member to walk the barriers again. When she or he bumps into one of these team members help the blindfold member to find a new path. Take him or her back to the beginning and watch how he or she walks – old habit or barely learned new habit?

Thank the volunteer (remove the blindfold) and lead the team in a discussion of habit in the workplace and how we can change it for the better.

CHAPTER 3

*T*HE TIME AUDIT

KEY LEARNING POINTS

- ■ **When time flies this is where it goes**
- ■ **My time usage affects your time usage**
- ■ **Work takes on different forms**
- ■ **The way we tackle a task affects the time a task takes**

INTRODUCTION

To find out what you really do with your time you need to conduct a time audit. A time audit is simply a very detailed diary of the time you spend and how you spend it. This chapter provides you with the necessary paperwork to conduct a time audit.

Make sure that every member of the team conducts a time audit on the same day; this way you will see the knock-on effect that one person's way of spending time has on another person in the team.

There are no special exercises to go with this chapter – the whole chapter is an exercise in itself.

WHY AUDIT TIME?

Do you really know what you do with your time? If, at the end of the day, you look up from your desk with no idea how your time has been spent yet you know that you have not achieved the list of items you intended to achieve, a time audit is for you. If your team does its best to work together but always seems to hit backlogs or periods when one person is waiting on another for the next task, you need to conduct a time audit. If you want to get the best from your time you certainly need to conduct a time audit because a time audit is the only way in which you can find out what actually happens to every 24 hours that pass. As a team it is far better to conduct the time audit together, on the same day. If you do this you'll understand the effect you have on each other and the effect that being in a team has on you. What is more, you'll see how time is really spent in the team and who wastes whose time. Be prepared to discover that the more senior the person the more likely they are to waste the time of people junior to them. Junior people's time will be wasted as they listen to group phone calls, wait for tasks and paperwork to be handed down to them, hover for the right moment to ask a question and generally wait for further instructions.

When we conduct time audits we find out many things about ourselves but, in order to learn, the truth is essential: if you spend half an hour looking out of the window you must write it down. And no one should condemn anyone else for the facts recorded in their time audit. Indeed it is probably not useful for team members to look at each other's time audit sheets; they need only to see the analysed results.

If you did spend half an hour looking out of the window, maybe your brain needed a rest, so maybe you are learning something about the way you work. Someone once reported on a time audit sheet that at 10.45 each morning she felt she needed a Mars Bar. 'I spent some time thinking about it ... I need a Mars Bar ... but that would make me fat so I can't have a Mars Bar. Maybe my blood sugar is low, I must eat something to rebuild'. Someone else in the room commented: 'I share an office with her – she doesn't just think it, she says it out loud, every morning at about the same time.' Well, her brain was definitely giving her a message: 'Take a break', it was yelling, loud and clear. The Mars Bar did not matter, eat one or not ... but what did matter was the need to stop work and take a break.

Sometimes all that is needed is to get up and stretch, sometimes we really need the break caused by going to make a cup of coffee or to run a page through the photocopier or even to take a walk around the office. Sometimes we even need the Mars Bar or the cup of coffee to recharge our batteries. In the UK people seem to feel they have to work all the time, very hard and for longer and longer periods. Some companies make a virtue out of working late and starting early, but our mainland European counterparts are very strict about not working so hard. They ensure that they only work the hours they are contracted to work. The laws covering employment hours are very strict and closely adhered to: even bosses go home at going-home time. It does not seem to limit their success, far from it.

Is that perhaps because they are more ready to work when it is work time and compared to our European counterparts we come to work already tired and hung over from the previous day's efforts?

Use the time audit sheets to find the answers to these questions:

1. When am I capable of my best work? Which really means, when should I never allow interruptions of any kind to my work schedule?
2. When does my brain need to take a natural break? How should I construct my day to take account of natural work patterns?
3. What do I actually do all day long?
4. How does the bulk of my time get spent?
5. Which members of our team are interdependent at particular times?
6. How can we best work together?

Conducting a time audit is an opportunity to talk about all the things that go wrong and right in the working day. It is also an opportunity to make sure that all the team members get the best out of their time. To grasp this opportunity to the full, choose a midweek day, a Tuesday, Wednesday or Thursday, and make sure that everyone fills in a time audit on the same day. It is best to ignore Monday and Friday because they can be atypical days and as a result bias the findings of the time audit. Allow everyone to complete an independent time audit and make sure there is no blame or criticism attached to what is written down. If the boss is wasting everyone's time it will not help the team to disguise the fact; it is better that we know it and can work with it.

Once the time audits are completed fix a meeting for about a week later to talk through the findings and to decide how the team can best benefit.

THE TIME AUDIT SHEETS

FIND OUT WHAT YOU DO WITH YOUR TIME

1. Take one typical day and analyse it in detail, describing what you do at quarter-hourly intervals using Figure 3.1.
2. About three days after the time audit, group and categorize the tasks listed on Figure 3.1 and transfer them onto Figure 3.2 and Figure 3.3 (page 31).
3. From Figure 3.2 decide on answers to the rationale of what you do, using Figure 3.4 (page 32).

Time	Activity
11.00	_____
11.15	_____
11.30	_____
11.45	_____
12.00	_____ etc.

FIGURE 3.1: Detailed time analysis – one representative day

4. Make a checklist of the problem areas, ready to plan to improve them using Figure 3.5.
5. About three to four weeks after your first audit, repeat the entire exercise, looking for improvement and confirmation of action needed.

GENERAL TERMS ANALYSIS

Seven activities consume time:

1. *Sleep* Including being brain-dead in meetings.
2. *Personal* Including gossiping, trips to the loo, lunch-time.
3. *Work travel* Including travel to and from your job as well as travel as part of the job.
4. *Domestic responsibilities* Gardening, shopping, housework, etc.
5. *Work* That you do.
6. *Self-development* Reading, keeping up knowledge, keep fit, learning a musical instrument or another language, etc.
7. *Leisure* Watching TV, playing golf, going out, socializing, etc.

On Figure 3.2, work out the percentage of the day in each category of activity.

Day	Activity (per Figure 3.1)	Percentage
_____		_____
_____		_____
_____		_____ etc.

FIGURE 3.2: General terms analysis

WORK TIME ANALYSIS

The work that we do can be looked at in a number of ways:

- *Progressive tasks* Move you forward.
- *Support tasks* Maintain status quo.
- *Reactive tasks* Reactions to others or situations that are not of your own making.
- *Destructive tasks* Ones that get you nowhere.
- *Constructive tasks* Ones that produce a result.
- *Panic tasks* Done without thinking.
- *Contemplative tasks* Done with thought.
- *Real tasks* Things that really merit being done.
- *Hobby tasks* Things we do because we like to do them or to put off doing other things.
- *Team tasks* Teamwork.
- *Solo tasks* Tasks done by yourself.
- *Urgent tasks* Failure to do them by a certain time negates the value of doing them at all.
- *Important tasks* Which matter to the organization and move it forward.
- *Habit tasks* Ones you do because you have always done them.
- *Instruct-a-task* Training someone else to tackle your tasks.

Your style of tackling those tasks can vary between:

- *Go it alone* It's quicker to do it myself.
- *Dump* Off-load and freeload.
- *Delegate* Hand over ownership of the task to another.
- *Empower* Enable someone else to tackle the task.
- *Share* Work together for the good of the organization.

Now look again at the time you have recorded as working time and analyse that time both as task style and tackling style. Remember a task may fall into several categories: it could be *urgent, panic* and *reactive* or maybe *important, progressive* and *real*. Use Figure 3.3 to complete this analysis.

Activity	Task style	Tackling style
		etc.

FIGURE 3.3: Work time analysis

RATIONALE

Common-sense tips are the best ways of saving time. But in order to give them, you need to be able to spot the wood from the trees. Read through your time audit sheets (Figures 3.1 to 3.3) and answer the eight questions in Figure 3.4.

1. What do I do that is *unnecessary*?

2. What do I do that others *could do better* (more economically or more effectively)?

3. On which things do I spend *too much time*?

4. How can I avoid *over-using* others' time?

5. Where can I make my most *important savings*?

6. On what do I spend *too little* time?

7. What are the *causes* of my time problems?

8. How can I organize *more cost-effectively*?

FIGURE 3.4: Rationale

TASKS AND TASK STYLES: THEIR EFFECT ON THE TEAM

In order to complete Figure 3.3 each team member would have thought about the work they accomplished and the type of task. The form in Figure 3.3 offered the task choices as listed in the accompanying section on work time analysis. Some of those tasks will always be constructive inasmuch as they will help to maximize the use of time, such as:

- progressive tasks
- constructive tasks
- contemplative tasks
- real tasks
- important tasks

Some will always be destructive inasmuch as they minimize the use of time and prevent other tasks from being tackled, i.e.

- reactive tasks
- destructive tasks
- panic tasks
- hobby tasks
- habit tasks

Figure 3.3 also looked at the way you might tackle a task. It suggested five key styles:

- go it alone
- dump
- delegate
- empower
- share

In today's world it is never quicker to do it all yourself. Each person needs to do their best and work to their strengths, which means using other members of the team to cover their weaknesses. All that happens if you try to do everything is that you get nothing done, frustrate others and cause knock-on time problems – but you do get to feel like a martyr. Actually your team members will also feel hard done by and will see you as greedy and unfair, so martyrdom does not even rest easy on your shoulders.

On the other hand, to dump a task on someone else is not right. We each have to make our contribution to the whole team; dumping means abdication of responsibility and failure to play our part.

Delegation is something else entirely. It means handing over ownership of a task while maintaining responsibility for that task. Delegation is what makes a job grow and allows individuals to develop; it also means that teams get the task done more effectively.

When you empower someone you give them the skills to tackle a task. This may be giving them training, by using this book as a development exercise for example, or it may be by paying for them to take external training. Empowerment and delegation given together mean that a team member is able to contribute at the highest possible level.

Sharing just means good teamwork – the kind of teamwork that recognizes and uses individual strengths for what they are, and does not allocate duties according to job title or rank but rather according to strengths and abilities.

WHAT DO WE DO NOW?

There is no point going to all the trouble of conducting a time audit if you ignore the results. The first thing you must do is to establish each team member's preferred time of day for working. We are mostly either morning people or afternoon people. Morning people do their best work in the morning and are happier free of interruptions at that time, afternoon people favour the afternoon. Make a chart listing who works best at which time and make sure that the workload is planned to accommodate these preferences. This makes sense and makes best use of time. Of course it may not be possible to stick to the preferences at all times but it will be possible most of the time with a little effort from the team. Chapters 4 and 7 give you some key tips to maximize the use of this prime production time.

Next establish the team's pattern: who interacts with whom. Of course there may be no surprises here but very often there are. Sometimes we have not truly realized who is having a knock-on effect on another person's work without realizing it. Is our team affected by other teams within the organization? If so, can we get them to work to a different time scale to help us maximize our time without destroying theirs?

Many people will have decided that they want to do something different as a result of the time audit. In Chapter 2 we looked at the powerful effect of habit and its hold on us. Get help from other team members to make that change. Figure 3.5 has a column for listing who will help you change and improve your use of time. Make sure you fill in the name of a team member to help, and make sure that you enlist that help, and that you help others who ask for help.

Activity	Need to change	Who will help

FIGURE 3.5: Checklist for time improvement

In the light of the information gained by this exercise the whole team may decide to change all or part of its way of working. If so, make a plan of what will change and make sure that every team member monitors the effect of the change. Then, once the change has begun to be established, conduct another time audit to see how things are going. It is best to let at least three to four weeks pass before conducting the second audit but that audit is in itself essential – essential to make sure that the actions you took were the right ones in the first place and that the desired effect is happening.

It will be very important to discuss the contents of individual Figure 3.4s as completed. These forms not only take account of the findings of the time audit but of the opinions of the auditors themselves. Questions 1, 2, 3 and 6 in Figure 3.4 will provide key answers to how the team works together. Question 7 can be very telling if anyone names someone else as a cause of time wasted. Equally, it is very important to know if you feel you overuse other people's time at question 4.

CHAPTER 4

PRIORITIZING – THE KEY TO IT ALL

KEY LEARNING POINTS

- Learn how to create instant mission statements
- Understand what urgency really means
- Understand the difference between support tasks and progressive tasks
- Discover a technique for controlling your day

INTRODUCTION

This chapter shows you how to teach your team to prioritize in a way that will help both you and your organization.

First, it looks at ways your team can create personal and team-based mission statements that will enhance the organization's own mission. Even if your organization has no mission statement you can still use a team mission statement to help you to make sure that your priorities work well. For those organizations with mission statements this section can be used to re-energize the mission and to personalize it.

The section on analysing tasks helps the team to differentiate between the various types of tasks each member undertakes. It will help them to see their jobs in a new light. It will also give each member of the team ways of explaining wheat you are doing when asked and you as team leader a way of making sure they tackle the right tasks at the right time. It is unlikely that any of you have analysed your tasks in this way before, so get the whole team to try out the theory together by using Exercise 4.2.

The chapter goes on to look at taking control over your life. Each team member probably thinks he or she is in control until crisis strikes or until a demanding person wants something. But none of us is really in control unless our lives are taking us along our chosen paths.

Finally, there are a number of exercises. You can use them as learning tools with the team or set them for individual team members to tackle alone to ensure that they have absorbed the key learning points of the chapter.

MISSION STATEMENTS FOR ALL

You may be tempted to see mission statements as a gimmick brought in from America to keep the bosses happy. Indeed some mission statements are too long and woolly to be of any use as a prioritizing tool. The characteristics of a good mission statement are:

- Everyone understands it.
- It is short enough for everyone to remember it.
- It explains what business the organization is in.
- It reflects achievable standards.
- Everyone believes in it.
- It reflects the values and beliefs of the organization.
- It emphasizes what the organization is good at.
- It answers the four key questions:
  - why the organization exists
  - what it exists for
  - who the main clients or customers are
  - how the organization goes about its business.

If your mission statement is written on a small card or key fob and respected by everyone in the organization, use it as your starting base. It will tell you where the organization is going and how it intends to get there. If there is no mission statement or you are unsure about its value as a prioritization tool, use the four key questions to help the team to build a team mission.

1. *Why are we here?* What is our main contribution to the world? How do we want to be remembered? What is our special or unique selling point?

    Example: My business is a training business. It developed

because I could not find the training I wanted. I believe training should be fun and practical, that it should be something people look forward to.

We are here to provide practical training workshops which are fun to take part in . . .

2. *What is our purpose?*   What is the product/service we produce? Why does the world need it? What do our customers/clients experience as a result of doing business with us?

   Example: My business exists to provide training courses in the field of practical management skills. It is necessary because schools and colleges and even professional qualifications do not provide the necessary practical learning and because new ideas develop after people leave education establishments or qualify. As a result of doing business with me my clients have new skills which they can immediately put to practical use.

   We are here to provide practical management skills training workshops which are fun to take part in . . .

3. *Who are our clients/customers?*   What type of organizations are they? Who are they? What do they want from us? Why do they buy the product/service we offer?

   Describe the team's customers/clients in terms of what they want. NB: If none of you is sure, the marketing department is paid to know and should be able to tell you. But don't be a drop-in visitor!

   If your team is based at head office or provides some kind of central service such as finance, remember that the customers/clients may well be other teams within the organization: help your team members to see that.

   Example: My clients want to spend as little money as possible on training and to get more productive people as a result. They want it cheap, they want it good. They spend money on training because they see it as a cost-effective way to match the team's skills to the needs of today.

   We are here to provide practical management skills training workshops which are fun to take part in and which represent good value for money for our clients . . .

4. *How does the organization achieve its purpose?*   In what way does it work? What are the key technologies used? Is the organization

ISO 9000 registered? What do the stakeholders or owners want from the organization? Describe what your organization wants and how it does what it does.

Example: I want to be successful and I equate that with making a profit while enjoying my job. I provide a quality service which I try to upgrade every year by using all the modern technologies available to me.

We are here to have fun while providing quality practical enjoyable management skills training workshops using the latest ideas and developments and which represent good value for money for our clients while making a profit for Jane Allan & Associates.

And that is my mission statement which helps me prioritize on the tasks I have to tackle. You could build a mission statement in much the same way. Try to make it fit into one sentence the way I have done; try also to make it sound sincere, something you will believe in and take to heart.

The next stage is to break the mission down into elements that represent the individual tasks of team members. Now you need to ask how the work of the department pursues the mission of the organization as a whole.

For example, in a training business the computer technology people make sure that the equipment is working and kept up to date. They train the users so that they can get the best from the equipment provided and they suggest any new ideas of which they are aware. They may not provide any external training courses but their customers are internal and if the internal customers get a poor quality service then the external ones will suffer too.

A good way for each team member to establish the key elements of his/her job in relation to the overall mission is to ask, 'What five key things could I do wrong which would result in the organization failing to meet its mission?' For example (staying with our computer department):

1. Fail to keep the equipment working properly so that the notes could not be produced.
2. Fail to install new programs correctly so that they crash and result in material being lost or late.
3. Ignore new developments so that the business falls behind its competitors in material production.
4. Refuse to help the user so that the user becomes bad-tempered and takes it out on the client. (Behaviour breeds behaviour.)
5. Forget to train the users who then fail to use the software to its

fullest extent and thus take longer producing the necessary material.

Once the team members have established clearly why they are here and what the organization stands for, they can examine each task on their desks to see if that task will help the organization achieve its purpose. For that matter, team members can prioritize each task within their job specifications and build a standard plan for tackling tasks.

Of course, there is an argument that if it has to be done then it is for the benefit of the organization. But everyone knows that this is not totally true. Some tasks benefit the organization more than others, some have a long-term effect, while for some the value lasts only for a few short hours. And of course the task that is so important to one department may not have equal value within the organization as a whole. Filling in forms may have the highest priority for the storekeepers but to the production team the forms are secondary to making the product. Both tasks are important to the organization as a whole but without the product there is no need for forms.

ANALYSE YOUR TASKS

No one needs any help in deciding whether reading a gardening magazine or getting on with the job is more effective for the organization. But what about the day-to-day tasks that need to be done and yet keep you from the big tasks? What about the man from accounts who screams and shouts and waves his arms about a lot in order to get what he wants before anyone else? Is doing his task first the right way to prioritize or is it just a search for a quieter life? The team needs a system which distinguishes between *importance* and *urgency*. Most individuals cannot make that distinction easily.

IMPORTANCE AND URGENCY

It is urgent so we'll take urgency first. Well, that is what most of us do. But who said it was urgent? And by what standards?

Rule number 1

Never let anyone else decide which of your tasks is the most urgent. Don't ask 'Is it urgent?'; there is bound to be one reply and one reply alone – 'Yes'. In translation this means 'It's mine so it must be urgent'.

So what does the term 'urgency' mean? Whatever your favourite dictionary says, use the following definition:

Failure to do something by a specified time renders doing it worthless.

Which means that you can have a task that is classified as urgent but that has, on 31 January 1996, a deadline of 16.00 on 14 September 1998. All this means is that the task is urgent but postponable for a while at least. Of course if the task is postponed until 15.00 on 14 September 1998 it will be very urgent indeed. So the team needs to establish degrees of urgency and prioritize accordingly. And that is simple: all team members need to do is to allocate a *must be done by* target to every task as they add it to their 'to do' sheet.

Importance isn't quite so simple. There are tasks that are straightforward, mundane even, and yet important to the organization. There are also tasks that are one-offs, perhaps risky and yet if they could succeed, very important to the organization.

SUPPORT TASKS AND PROGRESSIVE TASKS

A task is important if it helps the organization achieve its mission. A task can be both urgent (have a time limit) and important but it will fall into either support importance or progressive importance.

Support tasks maintain the organization where it is; they maintain status quo. In the accounts department such tasks might be preparing the monthly management accounts; for a manufacturer they might be maintenance of the machinery; in a shop, preparing for the day's sales by getting the displays right and setting up the till – all very valuable tasks, all important tasks in fact, but all tasks that serve only to maintain status quo.

On the other hand, if the accountant were to devise a new budgetary control system which completely revamped the monthly management accounts, giving access to interpretive information that was not available before, this would be progressive task. And if the manufacturer held a brainstorming meeting with his team to decide how to cut regular maintenance time and relieve bottlenecks, then that would be a progressive task. For the shopkeeper it might mean laying out the store to make it more conducive to impulse sales, or changing the products he sells to meet the changing customer profile. These tasks all move the organization forward in its quest to achieve its mission. They are important, just as the support tasks are important. No one type of task is more important than another, merely different.

Support tasks are much easier to justify than progressive ones. Others always understand what you are doing – it's your job, after all. Support tasks are predictable and tend to go right first time; this is because they have been done many times before. In my training organization such tasks could be represented as putting on a tried and tested workshop that has run many times before and achieved its objectives. It maintains my status quo and it is safe. But one day my clients may find another source of training that is more adaptable, perhaps more adventuresome, so at some stage I am going to have to spend time on the progressive tasks.

Progressive tasks take longer than support ones; they are new and risky and we do not know at the outset how they will proceed. Sometimes people wonder what we are doing, 'wasting all that time when there are urgent things waiting to be done'. But very often a progressive task can remove the need for any number of support ones in the future. Imagine the people working on our computer desk. Every day they receive cries for help, often the same cries for help, even from the same users. To maintain the status quo they will ensure they carry out the important support tasks of righting the problems and solving the queries. But what if they were to spend, say, two days thinking about the problems that occur regularly and then come up with a solution to them once and for all? Now that would be a progressive task indeed. Of course it is possible that the solution would not be that easy to find and then people would wonder why they were wasting their time. Perhaps the solution is glaringly simple, it just needed time to set it in context. Perhaps it is to publish a weekly list of the top 10 problems and their simple solutions and circulate it to all users. That is a progressive task – it moves the organization forward and frees up time for even more progressive tasks. But remember: it is risky, the team may not find the right solution quickly, the solution may not work and others (including bosses) may think the team has been wasting time when it could have been completing a number of support tasks.

Rule number 2

Sort all the team's tasks into support tasks that maintain status quo and progressive tasks that move the organization forward.

Now the team as a collective group should have six piles of tasks:

1. Urgent but unimportant
2. Non–urgent and unimportant
3. Urgent support tasks
4. Urgent progressive tasks
5. Non–urgent support tasks
6. Non–urgent progressive tasks

Begin by casting type 2 tasks into oblivion; they do not need to be done.

Next, consider the urgent but unimportant. Why have you categorized them like that? Why are they urgent? Is this a crisis? Is the urgency implied by the previous owner of the task? If so, recategorize. If the definition holds, and the urgency is immediate, then do them now but allow very strict time allocation for them.

Now turn to the urgent and important tasks. Categorize them on the team's 'to do' list and book slots for them in the relevant team member's diary, even if you are booking a slot some long way ahead.

Next, the non-urgent support tasks. Do they need to be done? Can they be delegated to someone with fewer time constraints? If not, list them and keep the list to hand. If team members are wise and leave enough time in their day to dream about making a million, these tasks will eventually get done and in good time.

I worry about the non-urgent progressive tasks. It is easy to put all progressive tasks into this category. It has a subtitle 'Nice but I have other things to do right now'. There is an old American Civil War rhyme:

> **For the want of a nail a shoe was lost**
> **For the want of a shoe a horse was lost**
> **For the want of a horse a rider was lost**
> **For the want of a rider the battle was lost**
> **For the want of a battle the war was lost**
> **And all for the want of a horse shoe nail**
> (Benjamin Franklin, *Preface to Poor Richard's Almanac*, 1758)

The replacement of the horseshoe nail was not urgent: after all, other nails were holding the shoe on. It was a support task if it had been spotted. But to set up a system to spot it, now that *was* a progressive task and no one got around to it!

So what does the team do if more than one task comes up on the list as having the same priority level and the same degree of urgency, yet it is not possible to achieve all the tasks in this category at the same time? Sometimes holidays will force this position upon the best-prioritized teams.

TAKE CONTROL OVER YOUR LIFE

To succeed in this world we have to know what we want. After all, if we do not know what we want, how will we know when we have it? Taking control of your life is simple: just write down on a piece of paper what you want from your life in five years' time. Now go for it!

Most of us find that list of things we want quite hard to write. The trick is to think big and then analyse small. Each team member should take a sheet of paper and write down the kind of things that matter to them. Those key things may be abstract, like harmony and peace. They may be difficult to define in a work environment, like blue sky and wheat fields. They may be very specific, like my boss's job. They may be smaller, such as to stay as I am and make fewer mistakes. They may be enormous, such as to enjoy life to the full. It does not matter what they are; anyone who has big thoughts can analyse them into smaller ones and see the effect they have.

At the end of this exercise team members will know what they want from life in five years' time. Next, each member of the team should go back to the list of tasks the team was trying to prioritize. Leave alone all those that have natural priorities, turn instead to the ones that have equal time and importance priorities and push to the front of the queue any task that will take individuals even just a few steps nearer to where they want to be in five years' time.

For team members, part of taking control over their own lives is taking control over their own diaries. This should work for each team member as an individual and as part of the team, not against them. Don't fall for the grand leather-bound systems of vast volume and detail if that is not the way your mind works. Here are some simple diary rules; live by them and the diary will help everyone, ignore them and it will turn into yet another hurdle team members have to cross daily.

Personal diary rules

1. Always keep one diary only.
2. Never carry more pages of your diary around than you need. When January is over tear it out and toss it away. Don't add September until you are booking dates in that month. In fact, don't carry your diary at all if you can avoid it. Keep it on your computer where the whole team can access it.
3. Get a diary big enough to write clearly. For me that means A4 page sizes with plenty of space. If your diary is on the computer make sure you can read each day clearly at all times.
4. Say thank you nicely for those grand diaries that are packed to the gunwales with useless maps and facts and then throw them away. Instead, run off a few sheets of A4 paper marked up as you need them to be. Figures 4.1 and 4.2 show two examples that work for

me – feel free to copy them for the team to use.

5. Use your diary to book time for you to do your job and then allow other people to book meetings in it.

8:00 am	**Tasks**
8:30 am	
9:00 am	
9:30 am	
10.00 am	
10.30 am	
11:00 am	
11.30 am	
12:00 pm	**Speak to/Write to**
12:30 pm	
1:00 pm	
1:30 pm	
2:00 pm	
2:30 pm	
3:00 pm	
3:30 pm	
4:00 pm	
4:30 pm	**Don't forget**
5:00 pm	
5:30 pm	
6:00 pm	
6:30 pm	
7:00 pm	
7:30 pm	
8:00 pm	

FIGURE 4.1: Diary – one day

APRIL

Monday	Tuesday	Wednesday	Thursday	Friday	Saturday	Sunday
		1	2	3	4	5
6	7	8	9	10	11	12
13	14	15	16	17	18	19
20	21	22	23	24	25	26
27	28	29	30			

FIGURE 4.2:   Diary – one month

Now let's take a further look at rule 5. It really means what it says: do not use a diary to book time for other people, use it to book time for yourself an then use it to allocate time to others for meetings. All each team member has to do is to decide how long he or she needs to get the job done. Remember the man who found he had only two days left to run his precision product factory after taking out all the time spent in meetings? Unless he worked a substantial amount of overtime he simply did not have enough time to get his job done. Never become like him – that way ruin lies!

Imagine a team member's job takes three and a half days a week to do well, that leaves just one and a half days for meetings. Be firm if the meeting quota is already taken up and move the next meeting into next week. But don't be silly, of course. If part of a team member's job is to run, chair or attend meetings then those meetings form part of the three and a half days.

Next, each member of the team needs to establish what kind of a person they are: a lark who works well in the mornings or an owl who never comes to life before lunchtime. The time audit will have helped with this but so will team members' habit studies and their knowledge of their upbringing. Quite frankly we all do our best and most time-effective work when our brains are at the peak of performance, so book out that time now. Try to make it sacrosanct, label it Key Personal Time.

Now each team member must establish what kind of a job he or she does. The job of a journalist involves meetings in the morning and writing in the later part of the day. So journalists have to allow meeting time in the mornings to be able to meet the organization's mission. Those who work in an international company will need to take note of world times when key colleagues or clients are awake and ready to do business. Once again each individual should mark out this time: call it Key Organization Time.

At last everyone can allocate the routine tasks such as opening the mail or dealing with routine matters. Don't worry if such tasks have not caught your prime time, after all they are not prime tasks and they will be done just as well in the slot allocated to them.

Figure 4.3 shows a diary marked out for someone who is a natural lark, with a job that takes three and a half days to accomplish, and who works in a European business that holds meetings over lunch.

Work out your own life pattern sheet and see how the complete team picture compares.

Monday 14 March	Tuesday 15 March
Keep free for crises	*Key Personal Time* *Progressive Tasks*
Free time	*Meetings*
Key Organizational time	*Free time*
Wednesday 16 March	Thursday 17 March
Key Personal time	*Key Personal Time*
Meetings	*Meetings*
Key Organizational Time	*Key Organizational Time*
Friday 18 March	Saturday 19 March
Key Personal Time *Progressive Tasks*	
Free time	Sunday 20 March
Keep Free for Crises	

FIGURE 4.3: Diary sheet for a particular type of individual

SUMMARY

If you want to use your time well you must prioritize. All the priorities you set should be your own and not ones that the previous owner of the job may have allocated to the task. Nor should you allow yourself to be influenced by people who scream and shout and wave their arms about a lot! This takes willpower but you will be able to do it if you know what:

- the organization's priorities are, and
- your own priorities are.

The rules of good prioritizing are:

1. First read the mission statement in order to understand the organization's priorities. (If there is no organization mission statement or it is not suitable for your purpose, create one in order to be able to prioritize effectively.)
2. Urgency means that failure to do something by a specified time renders doing it worthless.
3. Set your own levels of urgency.
4. A task is important if it helps the organization achieve its mission.
5. Support tasks are important tasks that maintain the status quo of the organization. They are part of your job specification, free of risk and they tend to go right.
6. Progressive tasks move the organization in the direction its mission statement says it wants to go. They are risky and may not result in success but when they do they move an organization forward.
7. Always begin by sorting your tasks into the six categories:
   - urgent but unimportant
   - non-urgent and unimportant
   - urgent support tasks
   - urgent progressive tasks
   - non-urgent support tasks
   - non-urgent progressive tasks.
8. Take control over your life: know what you want from it and use that knowledge to prioritize.
9. Take control over your diary by following the five basic rules:
   - one diary only
   - carry only the dates you need
   - get a big diary, write clearly
   - throw away useless information
   - book the time you need to do your job first.
10. Stick to your priorities once set, and change them only if you have further information.

EXERCISES AND THE LEARNING CONTRACT

At the end of this session your team members will have learned the importance of good prioritizing; they will also have learned how to ensure they prioritize their work in the interests of the organization as a whole, the team in particular and for their own personal good.

YOUR ROLE

Read through all the material in this chapter carefully, making sure that you understand it. Try and think of some examples that come from your organization which could enforce the learning message.

Exercise 4.3, Taking Control, is best done individually and alone but the results can be discussed as a team effort. It might be a good idea to ask individuals to work at it over a period of, say, one week and then get together to discuss the results. Make time for any queries or worries they may have while they are working on the exercise.

The purpose of these sessions is for your team to discover the art of prioritization, guided and helped by you but not told by you. Your role is to be a facilitator not a trainer. To achieve this you will need to make sure that the team is relaxed and ready to work together. Sometimes it is a good idea to clear the air before settling down to a session like this. Sometimes you may prefer to run an ice-breaker session to help people relax.

You must be prepared for the session, so after reading through the material get all the necessary kit together and make sure that you have a room in which to work where you will not be interrupted.

THE KIT

You will need:

- flipcharts (preferably one per three team members)
- plenty of coloured flipchart pens (not just one colour)
- Blu-tak™ so that you can stick the finished lists to the wall
- your lesson plan script
- copies of the overview for each participant
- instructions for each exercise

Some exercises require pre-prepared materials (the ice-breaker, for example) so make sure you have all the necessary kit prepared in advance by checking with the exercise each time.

THE CONTRACT

All training such as these sessions can be fun: it should be fun. We learn far more when we are relaxed and enjoying ourselves than when we are stressed or bored. Do make sure that the lessons are lasting ones, though. To do this you will need to agree a changed plan of action after the sessions, to draw up a team contract for improved working performance. Make your contract relevant to the results of each session, design it together with the team and agree to put it up on the wall where all can see it or even to add it to your procedures manual. Figure 4.4 is a typical contract sheet.

Team .... has run a session on ....

.... and as a result has agreed

to the following team rules:

Rule 1

Rule 2

Rule 3

Rule 4

All members of the team will work to our agreed rules.

Signed:

FIGURE 4.4: The team contract

Exercise 4.1 – Write a mission statement

You will need:

- flipchart paper
- pens
- space
- flipchart stand (four if possible)
- time: about 30–45 minutes.

Your purpose is to answer the four key questions, so write them up on four separate pieces of flipchart paper, one question per sheet.

1. Why are we here?
2. What is our purpose?
3. Who are our clients/customers?
4. How do we achieve our purpose?

Now take time to brainstorm the answers. Each person should write their ideas on the relevant sheet until all ideas are exhausted.

Now collect the ideas and tear them into strips so that each idea is on a separate piece of paper.

Next, pile the ideas one on top of each other to build a collection of ideas in the following categories:

- similar
- compatible
- incompatible
- good
- not so good
- attainable

Some ideas will fall into more than one category; write a second or third sheet and add them to the pile.

Finally, move the ideas around on a table or on the floor until you have a mission statement that will help you and your team prioritize.

Exercise 4.2 – Prioritize the in-tray

Ask each team member to make their list of priorities first and then discuss the completed lists in order to arrive at the team view.

You will need:

- flipchart paper
- pens
- flipchart stand
- time: about one hour.

You work for a pan-European organization with headquarters in the UK. You are Head of Administration and report to the Finance Director who is also responsible for administration. Your boss does not like dealing with administration matters. You have a team of people working for you, each responsible for administration in one section of the organization. They in turn have teams working for them. You also have a secretary. Today is Tuesday; yesterday you attended a time management course and now you are determined to make a change in the way you do things. On the course you discovered that you were a lark and that your organization's key time was from 11.00 to 16.00. Returning to your office you look at the pile on your desk and list the tasks as follows:

1. Two days' unread mail.
2. The minutes of a property meeting for approval.
3. Notes on the proposed new telephone system.
4. A fax from Frankfurt asking for guidance on installing a new filing system.
5. Your subordinate's report on the boiler replacement project.
6. Your plan – half completed about three months ago and then abandoned – to revamp the whole filing system throughout the organization.
7. Half-completed budget sheets for next year.
8. A memo from the Management Accountant asking for your completed budget sheets.
9. *Administration Today* – the latest issue with a very interesting article on filing systems for the future.
10. Four messages from the Head of Marketing complaining that the new desks that have been ordered are not of a high enough quality.
11. Twelve application forms for the post of Administrative Officer in the Bath office (the present incumbent leaves next month).
12. The report you commissioned on telephonic developments in the next ten years.
13. A memo from the reception team about suggested uniform changes and the problems caused by the shortage of telephone lines.

Your secretary enters and tells you she has fixed a meeting with the girls on reception for 11.00 today. She also reminds you that the board meeting is next Wednesday and you have to prepare a report giving your recommendations on the future of the telephone system in the UK (tasks 14 and 15).

The mission statement of your organization is:

> To provide a cost-effective, efficient and pro-active service to all clients while maximizing return to the stakeholders.

Using the diary sheet in Figure 4.5, plan the rest of your week and make a prioritized 'to do' list.

Monday 14 March	Tuesday 15 March
Time Management Course	
Wednesday 16 March	Thursday 17 March
Friday 18 March	Saturday 19 March
	Sunday 20 March

FIGURE 4.5: Sample diary sheet

Exercise 4.3 – Taking control

This exercise can only be done alone. It is to help team members discover and plan personal priorities. Although you may wish to discuss it in a team, this is not essential and you must respect the wishes of anyone who does not want to discuss their personal priorities.

You will need:

- a lot of paper or a computer
- a free and unhurried atmosphere
- as much time as it takes
- a clear and open mind.

Begin by emptying your mind of all the things that are cluttering it: just write them down in any order on a piece of paper. Now you can forget them, secure in the knowledge that when you need to remember them they will be there for you.

Next answer the questions in Figure 4.6, however daft they seem. Don't think too much about your answer, just let it flow.

Which of the four elements do I prefer? (Air, Fire, Water, Earth)

What is my favourite colour?

What do I enjoy most about my life?

Why do I do the job I do?

Do I enjoy the job I do? If not why not? If so why?

What do I dislike most about my life?

If I became very rich what would I do with the money?

Describe the kind of people you dislike most and like most.

Like

Dislike

FIGURE 4.6: Questionnaire to discover personal priorities

Then use the list of values in Figure 4.7 to help you decide what matters to you.

Now build your goal for this year, next year and five years' time. Build it further into the future if you wish.

Next, translate it into a personal mission statement using the same technique used earlier in this chapter.

It will then be there for you to use in setting your priorities.

Tick the items listed below that matter to you.

To get on in this world	❏	Innovation	❏
Honesty	❏	Winning	❏
Getting involved	❏	Looking out for oneself	❏
Working hard	❏	Obeying the law	❏
Cleanliness	❏	Democracy	❏
My parents	❏	My friends	❏
My children	❏	Patriotism	❏
Knowing one's heritage	❏	To be alive	❏
To build things	❏	To be free	❏
To save time	❏	Happiness	❏
To be right	❏	Wealth	❏
Success	❏	Religion	❏
Education	❏	To be accepted	❏
To know the right people	❏	To stand up for what you think is right	❏
To be productive	❏	To be tolerant	❏
To help people	❏	Beauty	❏

FIGURE 4.7: Values

Exercise 4.4 – Team diary match

The purpose of this exercise is to help team members prioritize together. It must be done after all the other exercises and can be used as a summary session.

You will need:

- flipcharts
- coloured flipchart pens
- a prepared OHP slide or flipchart or wallboard that maps out a day, another that maps out a week and a third that maps out a month.

Before the session, team members should make up their own daily, weekly and monthly diary plans, marking out key personal and organization time.

Ask team members one by one to put their time needs onto the communal charts. Try to use a different colour for each team member. Once all the plans are up and visible, look at any conflicting areas and see how the conflict can be resolved.

ANSWER TO EXERCISE 4.2

There is no perfect answer to any time management situation, only the one that works for you and your organization. Here is the one that would work for me. First the task categories:

1. Two days' unread mail – *urgent, may be important.*
2. The minutes of a property meeting for approval – *non-urgent, support.*
3. Notes on the proposed new telephone system – *progressive, urgent, see 15.*
4. A fax from Frankfurt asking for guidance on installing a new filing system – *progressive, see 6.*
5. Your subordinate's report on the boiler replacement project – *urgent, support.*
6. Your plan – half-completed about three months ago and then abandoned – to revamp the whole filing system throughout the organization – *progressive, see 4.*
7. Half-completed budget sheets for next year – *urgent, support.*
8. A memo from the Management Accountant asking for your completed budget sheets – *urgent, see above.*
9. *Administration Today* – the latest issue with a very interesting article on filing systems for the future – *progressive, see 4 and 6.*
10. Four messages from the Head of Marketing complaining that new desks ordered are not of a high enough quality – *support, not urgent.*

11. Twelve application forms for the post of Administrative Officer in the Bath office (the present incumbent leaves next month) – *support, urgent.*
12. The report you commissioned on telephonic developments in the next ten years – *progressive, see 15, 3, 13a.*
13. A memo from the reception team about suggested uniform changes – *support.*
13a. And the problems caused by the shortage of telephone lines – *progressive.*
14. Your secretary enters and tells you she has fixed a meeting with the staff on reception for 11.00 today – *support, non-urgent.*
15. She also reminds you that the board meeting is next Wednesday and you have to prepare a report giving your recommendations on the future of the telephone system in the UK – *urgent, progressive, see 12, 13a, 3.*

This answer is demonstrated in Figure 4.8 on page 58.

Although others, such as Head of Marketing, may have different priorities, certain things are not urgent for you. Do not be swayed by others' priorities.

You may be able to delegate certain items but assume for the moment that you cannot.

Monday 14 March	Tuesday 15 March
Time Management Course	*Scan read mail 1* *Approve boiler 5* *Finalize budget 7, 8* *Get secretary to contact* *Frankfurt, put on hold 4*
Wednesday 16 March	Thursday 17 March
New Telephone System *3, 12, 13* *Weed application forms* *Get secretary to fix* *appointments next week 11*	*Write Board Report 15* *Reschedule reception* *meeting 16.30 14*
Friday 18 March	Saturday 19 March
Take a fresh look at filing *system plan 6* *Read article 9* *Approve minutes 2* *Comfort Head of Marketing,* *get deputies to sort it out* *10*	Sunday 20 March

FIGURE 4.8: Diary sheet solution to Exercise 4.2

CHAPTER 5

PROCRASTINATION AND CAN'T SAY NO

KEY LEARNING POINTS

■ Practise active procrastination in order to stop it
■ Do something you dread: it is never as bad as you think
■ Nothing ever takes as long to do as to put if off
■ Saying no does not mean I hate you

INTRODUCTION

Everybody procrastinates. We all have our reasons but the most common reason for procrastinating is fear: Fear that something awful might happen or fear that when we start to tackle a task it will prove to be too difficult to accomplish. In this chapter we look at the part procrastination plays in your life and how you can minimize its effect while maximizing its usefulness.

Sometimes it is a good idea to procrastinate. It is a good idea to put off unimportant tasks until they go away. It is never a good idea to put off important tasks. Unimportant tasks often are the ones we seem to prefer to do. So procrastination even involves giving up the things you enjoy doing and doing instead the things that perhaps you don't enjoy. With the help of 'Procrastination party' (Exercise 5.1) – an exercise in controlling procrastination – you will be able to come to terms with the part it plays in your life and minimize its effect.

Because fear is a genuine part of procrastination and because each of us has the ability to be afraid of something or someone, this chapter also looks at the effect of fear and how to control it. A simple checklist helps each of us decide what the fear is and whether it is genuine.

Of course, sometimes the fear is of a boss or an individual to whom we want to say no but cannot. It is possible to say no even to your boss and even to your boss's boss. When you have problems saying no, it is usually because you imagine that by saying no you will be rejecting the individual. However, when you say no you very rarely reject the individual; perhaps if you have turned down a proposal of marriage then this is a rejection of the individual, but in our working lives saying no simply means 'I'm not able to do the task you require me to do at this moment in time'. It does not mean 'I hate you and hope you die of ptomaine poisoning overnight'. The very best way to say no is to do so constructively and in such a way that your counterpart does not feel personally offended or affronted. We shall look at a number of ways to say no which are in themselves helpful and constructive.

Two further exercises in this chapter (Exercises 5.2 and 5.3) give us an opportunity to practise new-found skills.

THE PART PROCRASTINATION PLAYS IN YOUR LIFE

So you procrastinate ... we all do. You know you have a task to do and you are not quite sure where to start, so you don't start. After all, if you leave it for a while you will have greater opportunity to think out different ways of starting. Take a look at your in–tray or at the piles of paper scattered around your desk (those papers won't be scattered around your desk after you have read Chapter 6).

- Are there any items in your in–tray or on your desk that have a curly corner and a coffee stain? If so, they are the subject of your procrastination.
- Are there any hidden things tucked away in the drawers of your desk?
- Any piles of reading matter gathering dust on the shelves?
- Any files that have dwelled in your briefcase travelling to and from work?
- Is your in–tray remarkably full and have the things in it been there for quite some while?

Item	Why is it there?	Real reason
		etc.

FIGURE 5.1: Analysis of items

If you can answer yes to any of these questions then you are talking about items over which you procrastinate.

In order to cure procrastination we have to first establish exactly what we are procrastinating over and why the procrastination is happening. So begin by taking all the items that are in your in-tray, on your desk, buried in the drawers of your desk, deep in your briefcase or in piles around the room, and make a list of them – a list that is very simple and looks like Figure 5.1.

In the 'Item' column describe the task that is waiting to be tackled. If there is more than one element to the task, list it in two places. Then in the 'Why is it there' column explain why the task is still waiting. Perhaps you are waiting for information from someone else; perhaps it is waiting because other tasks have been more urgent; perhaps it is waiting because you don't want to do it. Finally, in the 'Real reason' column there may be a need to put an entry to explain why it really is there. For example, perhaps you have a task on your desk which is ostensibly waiting for information from someone else but you know you could have chased for it and you know you *should* have chased for it. Maybe in this case the real reason is that you don't want to tackle it or that to tackle it will force you to have to do something else you don't like. Some of us don't like using the telephone and if tackling a task means that we will have to ring someone we don't enjoy talking to on the phone, then that task may well be put off for longer than necessary. Remember the only purpose for writing down and recording your real reason is to help you establish why you are procrastinating.

If you keep a detailed time audit of your work every day of your working life you will soon see how long it takes you to find reasons to put off a task. Let's imagine you pick up a task perhaps four or five times during a week and spend, say, five minutes looking at it and thinking about it, and then another ten minutes justifying why you can't tackle it right now. That amounts to one and a quarter hours.

Now add on the time you spent worrying about the fact that you should have done the task but haven't done the task and you will probably add on another half an hour. Next, add on the time you spend justifying out loud either to yourself or to others as to why the task hasn't been tackled, and let's be fair and say that's another quarter of an hour per day for a week, and we end up with three hours so far. Sometimes you will have to add on the time you spend making up and giving excuses for not having tackled the task, and let's estimate that at half an hour. Our grand total is three and a half hours trying not to do a task. How many tasks in that procrastination pile would take less than three and a half hours to accomplish? Or let me put it another way: nothing ever takes as long to do as it takes to put it off.

Now look at your end column in your list of procrastinated tasks. How many of them are put off because:

- You hate to do them?
- You are afraid of the consequences of the task?
- You don't know how to do them?
- You don't enjoy doing them?

HATE

Why do you hate the task? Is it something you have done in the past and it has bored you? Is it something you have done in the past and it has gone wrong? What do you associated with the task that makes you hate it? Do you associate pain? Do you associate personal irritation and frustration? Or do you simply have to work with people who you do not like? Is this a case of dealing with difficult people? Only you can analyse why you hate a task.

If you really thoroughly hate a task you should ask yourself whether you are the right person to be tackling it long-term. This may mean you have to tackle the particular version that is on your desk now but that you can subsequently delegate any further runs of the task. Meanwhile, the best way to tackle a task you hate is to bribe yourself. 'If I do this task now and get it done within the next half an hour then I can':

- do something else I prefer
- take a break
- reward myself with a Mars Bar
- feel exceptionally pleased with myself.

Another tactic is to tell yourself that you do not hate the task – that you thoroughly enjoy it. Sometimes there are tasks that the first time we tackle we do dislike but as we do them more and more often we suddenly find that they are actually quite pleasant after all.

AFRAID OF THE CONSEQUENCES

In the next section of this chapter we look specifically at dealing with fear. If you are afraid of the consequences of a task it must mean that you are fully aware of the potential consequences. If you are not aware of the consequences but just experience a general fear relating to the task, the first and most essential thing to do is to make a detailed list of what exactly it is you are afraid of. When you have completed that you will need to turn to the section of this chapter that deals with conquering fear.

HOW

If someone else in your team knows how to tackle the task, ask them to explain it to you. Make sure they explain it properly, so check that they have read Chapter 9 on the subject of delegation. If no one in your immediate team knows how to tackle the task then perhaps someone else in the organization does or perhaps the organization runs a relevant training workshop. If no one in the organization knows how to tackle the task then maybe you are going to have to find a workshop for yourself. Or perhaps there is another book in this series which will help you tackle a particular task. Never be afraid to admit that you don't know how to do a task; it is only when we admit that we do not know how to do something that people give us the necessary knowledge we lack. It is worth remembering, though, that there are some tasks that no one knows how to tackle until a way is found.

ENJOY

We spend a large part of our lives in the workplace. Of course it is important to enjoy our time at work, but we have to accept that there will be tasks that we don't enjoy and yet are essential tasks that have to be done. Whenever I have to tackle a task I don't enjoy, I reward myself with the same kind of bribes that I offer myself with a hated task.

An alternative method of reward is to make the task enjoyable. Perhaps this is the task you can accomplish in a different way or in a different venue. Maybe you would enjoy working at home – is this a task you could take home and work on one morning? Perhaps you are lucky enough to work in an office that is in a country area – maybe this is a task you could take outdoors in the summer and work on. Perhaps you want to learn a particular piece of computer software and haven't had the opportunity. Is there a way you can adapt this task so that in accomplishing the task you also learn a piece of software?

The best example I can think of for this is the individual who was asked to write a 1000-word essay for me on the subject of the future. I don't think he wanted to do the essay and I don't think he really felt he ought to be tackling it at all. However, all the key managers, of which he was one, in his organization had been asked to write this essay. At the time, he wanted to learn Powerpoint, the software presentation package, so he wrote his presentation in Powerpoint. This meant that he accomplished the unloved task and handed in his essay. And it also meant that he learnt Powerpoint and got some enjoyment out of the exercise.

This book is about looking for people's strengths; remember this and try not to make looking at weaknesses a witch-hunt. Obviously it is both time- and cost-effective to enable people to work to their strengths and not to have to utilize their weaknesses. In fact it is fair to say that the tasks you enjoy most are usually the tasks you are good at, and those tasks get done in preference to other tasks. The tasks you dislike doing, on the other hand, often sit around in a pile your in-tray. Maybe the reason you dislike doing these tasks is because you are not good at them and they represent areas of weakness on your part. If that is the case, the first thing you should consider is to delegate those tasks. Is there someone else in the team who is better equipped to tackle them and would be happier to tackle them? Go through your list of procrastinated tasks and see whether any of them can be delegated. If they can, Chapter 9 gives helpful advice on delegation.

Quite probably a large number of your procrastinated tasks cannot be delegated. Indeed, if you could have delegated them maybe you would have done so by now. For a lot of us, getting started is really the problem – once you have started on a task you can keep going. The biggest problem is starting at the beginning. Years ago, when everything was done on typewriters and handwritten or dictated, every letter, every report, every book had to start at the beginning, continue until it reached the end and then stop. But now that is not true: with the computer you can start anywhere you like, in the full knowledge that you can add material at the front, the end, the middle or anywhere else you wish. So the first piece of advice is never to try to start at the beginning. Start somewhere, anywhere that you fancy. Remember that old rule in exams: you were always advised to tackle first the question that you liked best or found the easiest, then when your energy was flowing you could deal with the more difficult questions. Well, treat your procrastinated tasks in this way. Start somewhere, anywhere, and see how you progress.

Perhaps you should start at the end with an idea of where things should conclude and work backwards to justify your conclusion.

Maybe you should start with a diagram, if you like drawing diagrams, or maybe with a chart, if you enjoy the chart program on your computer. Possibly you should start by writing the main body of a report, but not from the beginning of the main body – rather, from somewhere in the middle, wherever your knowledge is at its best. The key point is to let your starting generate the energy for you to continue.

Anyone who sits at a desk that is covered in paper will have an opportunity to procrastinate. Somewhere in those piles of paper is something:

- *Interesting* more interesting at least than the task you are tackling.
- *Urgent* but probably not important.
- *Fascinating* inasmuch as it looks exciting or colourful.
- *Worrying* inasmuch as it is a task that you should have done before the one you are doing now, because it is yet another task that you have procrastinated over.

Sweep the desk clear of all of these pieces of paper. Don't throw them away – keep them but put them in piles out of sight. If you follow the advice of Chapter 6 you will end up with a nice clear desk. Onto your nice clear desk, which contains only your computer, your telephone and your coffee mug, you can now place the piece of work that you are going to tackle. It is very difficult to procrastinate about a piece of work if the only document on your desk is the piece of work over which you are procrastinating.

Go the whole hog: make your procrastination deliberate. Sit back in your chair, lean back, maybe even put your feet on the desk, and if anyone asks you what you are doing, say 'I'm procrastinating'. Even if nobody asks you what you are doing you will soon feel silly and a little uncomfortable and settle down to find something to do.

One of the most common reasons why we all procrastinate is fear. Fear of failure and fear of the unknown. Sometimes it is even fear of the known, fear of the temper of someone for whom we are trying to accomplish a task, or fear of an individual who always makes us feel uncomfortable or small. That fear can be genuine, and fear certainly stops us performing at our best. The next section of this chapter looks at how we can conquer fear.

HOW TO CONQUER FEAR

Fear of the consequences of tackling a task is genuine. Each of us is quite capable of feeling a very real and honest fear of what might happen as a result of admitting that a task is completed. It could be that some tasks bring problems with them. So the very first thing you have to do if you feel that there is an element of fear in your procrastination is to try to analyse why you are afraid. Fear is likely to fall into the following categories:

- *Fear of the known* The last time you tackled the task something absolutely terrible happened. Perhaps you made a mistake, perhaps the task went wrong or perhaps the individual for whom you were working was intolerant or unhelpful. Maybe you think you know what will happen when you admit this task is completed. Some of us who suffer from fear of the known have a tendency to avoid finishing the task. We say to ourselves that it is not yet complete, that more work is essential and that we cannot therefore release it. This of course postpones the dreaded day when we have to admit the task is completed and that feared event takes place.

- *Fear of the unknown* Most of us experience fear of the unknown at sometime. This doesn't mean fear of ghosts or extra-terrestrial beings; it simply means fear of what might happen, which we can't predict but which we have a horrible feeling will not be as nice as what is happening now. This is roughly akin to changing your job. You choose to change your job, you applied for the new job, but on the first day there was an element of fear as you wondered what the new company would be like and how your new colleagues would react to you.

- *Fear of failure* If your organization is one that experiences 'blame culture', whereby individuals look for someone else to blame rather than admitting responsibility themselves, then you are very likely to experience fear of failure. Failure to you will mean punishment or at the very least a falling from the high opinion your colleagues may have of you. Some people have not yet failed in their lives. The more you succeed, the harder failure becomes. If I pass all my exams, pass my driving test, get accepted for jobs, achieve at all levels and rise to high status within my organization, not making a mistake or committing a failure until I have reached board director level, you can imagine how disproportionate that failure will feel to me. On the other hand, if I am someone for whom things regularly go wrong I will have that sinking feeling of 'Oh no, not again'.

Fear of failure can often encourage failure. Many years ago I worked with someone who was constantly pointing out the error of individuals' ways. As a result, things went wrong when we were around him. He was the kind of man that, if you stood in front of him holding a Ming vase in your hands, would automatically say 'Be careful you don't drop that' and your hands would spring apart allowing the vase to fall to the floor. Fear of his personality brought about fear of failure.

■ *Fear of people*   If only everyone would smile. Look around you in the office and you see people looking stern, serious, worried. Perhaps some of these people have those fixed expressions on their faces that make them look as though they are very miserable indeed. They are the kind of people you would not stop in the street to ask directions when you were lost. Their faces make you afraid. Some people peer over the top of half-moon glasses, others look up when distracted and instead of saying 'Can I help?' or smiling, just grunt and that grunt seems aggressive. Now imagine each of those individuals of whom you are afraid stark-naked on the lavatory. This was Winston Churchill's trick. When faced with an audience he felt fear, like any presenter. To quell that fear he imagined his audience seated stark-naked on the lavatory. As he said: you can't be afraid of people in that condition. If you don't want to imagine them in such a drastic position then ask them to smile – or even say something to make them smile. Perhaps smiling at them yourself will get a smile in response. When people smile some of the fear goes away.

These are the problems, the fears: treatment is easier than you think.

FEAR OF THE KNOWN

You have tackled this task before and you know the consequences. The consequences bring fear into your heart. Let us examine what that fear might be:

■ Will you be dead or maimed at the end of the task?
■ Will your house be burnt down or your possessions destroyed?
■ Will someone shoot your dog or eat your goldfish?
■ Will you be thrown into prison?
■ Will you be bankrupted?

If any of these are genuine and logical consequences of the task over which you are procrastinating, then you are quite right to procrastinate and I suggest never tackling the task again. However, for the majority of us these are not the consequences of tackling the task. Just making a list of them in that way may help you to get your fear into proportion. Write down exactly what your fear is and why you dread the consequences.

Does it involve an individual? If so, try to talk to the individual concerned; establish how he or she feels about the task and how important it is to that person.

Does your fear involve an event? If so, try not to allow the event that occurred last time to reproduce itself. For example, perhaps you could start the task from a different angle or work on it in a different venue. Perhaps you learned the lessons of last time and will ask for more information at the start. In any case, fear of the known is easy to deal with. You know what the consequences of the action are and you can analyse them. If we analyse things in very great detail we often analyse them down to the absurd. Once your fear is absurd you will be able to wipe it out.

FEAR OF THE UNKNOWN

This isn't quite so easy to conquer. First you should run through the same list of items that we checked above.

- Will you be dead or maimed at the end of the task?
- Will your house be burnt down or your possessions destroyed?
- Will someone shoot your dog or eat your goldfish?
- Will you be thrown into prison?
- Will you be bankrupted?

Once again, these fears will very likely be untrue. You are merely unsure of what might happen and discomfited when you are working without knowledge. So what you need is knowledge. Is there anyone who can tell you about the consequences or the outcomes of a task? Is there anyone who can give you further information? Has anyone else experienced it or is there a book published on the subject? What material is available in your library? Does the task have any parallels in your work or home life? Very often a task we have to tackle at work does have parallels at home. For example, if you have to find a way round a particular problem, perhaps because a resource is in short supply and you have to find a substitute, how will you tackle it? What are the consequences of not tackling it? Well, perhaps at home your child comes to you and tells you that it's sports day tomorrow and he hasn't got the necessary kit. Without the kit he can't take part in sports day and that is going to upset him. The shops are shut, you can't go out and buy new kit, and in any case you couldn't afford it. Is there some way you can make up that kit or is there someone from whom you can borrow it? I am sure in your personal life you will hit just these problems and solve them.

One small boy announced at eight o'clock one morning, when he was due to leave the house in 40 minutes, that he had to make a pizza at school. Unfortunately, he had forgotten to forewarn his parents that he would have to take in some cheese, a tin of tomatoes and a pizza base. Now there was not a pizza base or a tin of tomatoes available in the house. There was cheese but not the sort the boy liked. Casting all blame to one side his parents leapt to find solutions. Both of them went out to work so neither of them could solve the problem immediately, so they divided the solution. His mother went to the shop, purchased the necessary ingredients and took them to work with her. Her husband collected the ingredients from his wife at work and took them to the school where he delivered them to his son during a break. Quite what they did to the boy afterwards for forgetting remains undocumented, but the problem was solved and the resources were collected.

Perhaps you can tackle the unknown in a similar way if you are looking for a scarce resource; maybe more than one person could be involved in acquiring it and delivering it.

FEAR OF FAILURE

Failure is one of the most positive things that any of us experiences. Without failure we would not have Post-it™ notes. Without failure I would not enjoy the lifestyle I do today. Post-it™ notes are made with a glue that, when initially manufactured by 3M, was not suitable for the task for which it had been designed. It was a failure – a very profitable failure, as it happens. I began my working life as a secretary and I was a complete failure at it. I then became a chartered accountant and a partner in a firm of accountants and was not very good at that either. They got rid of me as a partner: failure twice. And yet today I run a very successful business providing training workshops and writing books. I enjoy my life and I enjoy my income so I don't regard those failures as having defeated me: rather, as having set me up for my success.

It is very hard to view failure in this way if your company does have a blame culture. But if you are part of an achievement culture and your organization recognizes the value of learning, then you will have been encouraged to report your failures. When things go wrong we have something to learn. What we learn we can utilize. If I do a task wrongly I will learn a number of things:

- how to put it right
- the consequences of doing it wrong
- how to do it right

If I always do the task correctly I will only learn how to do it correctly. I will not be ready to deal with any emergencies or indeed to adapt to the way the task is tackled. Failure leads to learning and learning leads to development and growth. Development and growth is essential if an organization is to be ready to meet the 21st century head on. Failure is a good thing. Do not be afraid of it but embrace it as your friend and use it to build your strength.

FEAR OF PEOPLE

Some people can be very unpleasant. Some people are actually hostile towards you – hostility whereby they wish to embarrass you, humiliate you and cause you to suffer. Now, unless you earn your living as a politician or preaching religion on street concerns, you probably don't experience much hostility. You may think you do, but what you are really experiencing is difficult situations: people asking you difficult questions or explaining things in difficult ways. Face the difficulty and ask them to repeat it in a different way, or reply to their question with another question that seeks a more detailed explanation of what they need to know.

Remember: hidden behind a serious expression, a worried look or an unhappy face is often a very pleasant person who is concentrating hard on the task in front of him or her. Remember, too, that senior people in organizations were junior people once and sometimes can even remember what it was like. Nor should you forget that the higher up a ladder you climb the tougher it is to fall. The more senior I am in an organization the more visible I am and the more concerned I am to make sure my contribution is the best. When that happens I may be abrupt and difficult when dealing with others. But beneath it all I'm a human being. Only be afraid of a person who can genuinely harm you. Very few people in your workplace can genuinely harm you.

TREATING FEAR GENERALLY

There is another way to deal with the unpleasant task that has brought about this fear and that is to tackle it bit by bit and in short time segments. For example, imagine there are at least four hours before the task will be completed and you must do it by Friday afternoon. I suggest an hour on Monday afternoon, half an hour Tuesday morning, an hour Wednesday afternoon and perhaps half an hour on Thursday afternoon will ensure that the task is done with plenty of time to review it on Friday morning. You won't have spent four miserable hours struggling through an unhappy task and you will have had the reward of feeling that it is being accomplished. If the task is very complex, break it down into smaller steps and focus on one step at a time. Perhaps that step is in itself far easier to work on than the complex combination of steps. Whatever you do, make sure that the small task you tackle gets you moving in the right direction to accomplish the complete task.

When you are trying to talk yourself out of fear give yourself a pep talk. Tell yourself how good you are, how you will not possibly fail, how the known only relates to last time and how the unknown will pale into insignificance. Tell yourself that you are an important person and that you have a contribution to make. Don't be a perfectionist – very few tasks require absolute perfection. The majority of tasks need to be accomplished and the accomplishment can sometimes be more important than the perfection standard. Of course this does not mean that you should produce shoddy work or work below agreed standards, but it does mean that if you can tackle a task and get it moving, your fear of producing a less than perfect task will be placed in proportion.

Finally, when it comes to fear don't wait to get yourself into the right mood. Don't say to yourself 'I'll feel braver tomorrow' or 'I'll feel better about it on Tuesday'. Start in spite of your mood. Tell yourself that the task when completed will improve your mood.

SAYING NO CONSTRUCTIVELY

Do you want your colleagues to like you? Or don't you care what they think? Most of us are concerned that our colleagues should at the very least be pleasant to us and probably that they should like us. But this can become a burden. It's very difficult to give negative replies or information to someone who you hope will like you. In fact, if we seek the approval and affection of others too eagerly we often lose their respect.

Perhaps the reason you don't say no is because you genuinely want to help other people. You are a nice person. You are concerned about the welfare of others and you would like to make their lives more pleasant and easier; beware, you may be taken for granted. I run my business from a village. It is a small and reasonably close-knit Hampshire community where lots of people are involved in many things. Living in the house opposite me there used to be a lady who volunteered for everything. She was secretary to this club, treasurer of that; if someone needed their shopping collected she would volunteer as a matter of course. If someone needed a lift into town she would gladly give them a lift into town. In fact she took on so many tasks that it became impossible to accomplish them in the time available. Yes, she got them done but she got everything done late. Now what did people say about her? Was it:

How kind of her to get all these tasks done?

Oh no, it was rather:

She was late with that again you know, oh you can't rely on her.

On the other hand, I volunteer for nothing. But every now and then a task comes my way which is possible for me to do within my schedule and then I say yes. This is rare but when it happens I am rewarded by a box of chocolates, a bottle of wine, even maybe a bottle of champagne, and certainly a note of thanks. Because, you see, by taking on just a few tasks I get them done on time.

Do not be afraid of offending people when you say no. You are not rejecting the human being. You are merely indicating that you don't have time available to accomplish the task they are asking you to do at present. In the process, however, be careful not to say no in such a way that implies that if the requested were to press harder with the request you would eventually give in.

The people to whom we need to say no in a work environment divide into a number of categories:

- *Your boss* who has perhaps asked you to do one task too many.
- *Your boss's boss* who is perhaps asking for a special favour or demanding an urgent piece of work.
- *Your colleagues* who want you to help them out.
- *People from other departments* who are seeking your advice or help in solving a problem.
- *Anyone* who is simply dumping a task on you.

Of course your response will need to be different when dealing with each of these five categories of people who are trying to encourage you to take on an extra task. The way you say no to your boss and your boss's boss may well be different from the way you say no to your immediate team colleagues. The way you say no to another department will have a lot to do with the way you might say no to an external customer. But the way you say no to the dumpers might be a lot firmer and even somewhat critical of their request.

SAYING NO TO YOUR BOSS

Very few bosses are unreasonable. Some are forgetful, some are bad at time management themselves and some are over-ambitious as to how time can be consumed. Forgetful and over-ambitious bosses are easy to handle, particularly if they are reasonable individuals. Do remember that most of us are reasonable individuals at heart.

Imagine that your boss has just asked you to do the fifth task that he seems to require to be completed by Friday afternoon. You know you can accomplish four tasks but you realize that to accomplish the fifth will put too much of a strain on you and the rest of your department. What do you say? Well, body language is important here too and this is exactly what you do.

First, think about the tasks you have to accomplish and as you think check them off on your fingers. It is not necessary to say anything at this stage but it is important to look as though you are thinking. Perhaps a frown, your head on one side or even muttering to yourself. Now you say:

That's the fifth task you need me to do by Friday afternoon. Perhaps you were not aware that we still had ...

and list the four that are outstanding.

I know that I can get four of these tasks done. Which one would be best for me to leave until Monday?

The boss who replies 'I want it all done now' will be a fool. I don't suppose you work for a fool, I imagine you work for someone who is quite reasonable and more likely to reply 'Oh I didn't realize that I had given you so much to do. X can help you', or possibly 'Leave this task until Monday; it can wait'.

Another way to say no to your boss and even to your boss's boss is to say:

I can certainly get that task done for you but it will mean taking some shortcuts on other tasks or perhaps leaving something partially completed. Are you happy with that?

This gives your boss an opportunity to weigh up the situation and to re-prioritize for him or herself. Most people appreciate that and most people are reasonable enough to prioritize sensibly. Indeed, it will even help here if you create prioritized lists on sheets of paper and make sure your boss knows your order of prioritization for your tasks.

If you work for more than one boss, or if your boss's boss frequently gives you tasks, you will need to make sure that you do keep some kind of list so that you are aware of who is asking you to do what and that each of the people who can allocate tasks is aware too. I think it is a good idea to keep such lists posted on the wall on a whiteboard in your office but at the very least keep them on the computer where they can be looked at by everyone conveniently.

SAYING NO TO YOUR BOSS'S BOSS

Sometimes your boss's boss bypasses your boss and asks you to do a task. Maybe you regard this as your being selected as someone important, maybe you look upon it as a nuisance. Whichever way, when you are asked to do a task by someone who is even more senior than your boss, it feels like a very important task. So ask just that question:

How important is this task to you? Would you like me to drop everything that I am doing now for [name your boss] **or should I put it onto the pile of tasks? Please help me to make the right decision for you.**

In translation, what you are really saying is: could we please talk, you, me and my boss direct, so that we can decide the exact order of priorities. Most bosses' bosses will be happy to do this because it is in their interest to ensure that the hierarchy does work and that tasks are accomplished that are necessary for the whole organization.

SAYING NO TO COLLEAGUES

Colleagues will often play upon your good nature by asking you to do them a favour. They might even say things like 'Just for me . . .'. Well, maybe you are happy to do something for a friend or a colleague but make sure that by doing it you are not harming your own task list nor getting a reputation as someone who is an easy touch. The best way to avoid this is to establish the key areas of your job and the key task that must always be accomplished. To do this is quite simple. Take a sheet of paper and write down five or more things that you have to do within your job – things that if you were to do wrongly or not do at all would cause hell to freeze over and a plague of newts to descend upon the earth. In other words, we are looking for tasks that are absolutely crucial to your job. Make a list of those tasks and make sure there is always time to do them during the day. Certainly make sure that you do not put these tasks off in order to help someone else. Once you have established these key areas and tasks then you have extra time, some of which you may be able to use to help your colleagues.

However, there will be a large number of occasions when you have to say no to colleagues. Here are some phrases that you might like to use:

- **I'm not very good at that – you need someone who could do it better than I can.**
- **If only you had asked me yesterday. Of course I could have done it but now I have committed myself to doing something else.**

- **I'm working on an urgent task at the moment for ....
  Please ask me another time when it will be easier for me to
  help you.**
- **Oh dear, I'm so busy at the moment that I really could not
  give the time that you need to this particular task. Have
  you tried asking ...?**
- **Certainly I can do that for you – could you do this task for
  me in exchange?**
- **Yes I would love to help – I haven't got time at the
  moment so would next Thursday be ok?**

Of course, with the last of these suggestions you will have to make
sure that you don't lumber yourself with a task on Thursday that you
have no intention of accomplishing!

SAYING NO TO OTHER DEPARTMENTS

Other departments will be your customers or suppliers. So if you are
in a position to say no to them you will need to think about how you
would say no to an external customer or supplier. When we say no to
external customers we need to make the customers feel that they
have said no to themselves. There are certain phrases that are like a
red rag to a bull when dealing with a customer; these include:

- **I can't do that.**
- **Company policy won't let me do that.**
- **You will have to, you must ...**
- **The computer prevents me from ...**

The way you say no to customers is to accentuate the positive and
play down the negative. If they want you to do something by
Thursday but you believe you can do it instead by the following
Monday, you begin by saying 'Well, I can certainly get that done for
you by Monday afternoon'. You have emphasized the positive
without drawing attention to a negative element and it is very likely
that they will accept your new deadline of Monday afternoon.
Imagine that a customer has rung in on the telephone and come to
the wrong department. You would say something like:

- **Let me help you to find the person who can tackle this for
  you.**
- **Let me give you the extension of the right person to ring.**
- **I'll put you through to the right person.**
- **Let me take a message and have someone ring you back.**

All of these suggestions are negative in themselves; they are actually saying 'no I cannot do this for you' but they are saying it in such a positive way that the customers feel they are being helped. Try these tactics on your colleagues.

SAYING NO TO DUMPERS

A very dear friend of mine is a very kind and generous person who always wants to help other people achieve the best for themselves. If you had a task that you didn't want to do, all you needed to do was to go to him and ask him how to tackle the task; he would always explain it to you. During the explanation, if you looked confused or worried, he would explain it again. Once the second explanation was completed you only needed to look worried again and this time he would say 'Well, let me just start it for you'. If you didn't allow your face to break out into a grin but merely continued to look confused and worried, eventually he would say 'Well, just this once I will do it for you'. I saw an endless succession of people walking away from his office with grins on their faces, having upwardly delegated a task they simply didn't want to do. He needed to learn to say no.

If you are in that position, the very best approach when someone comes to you querying the way to tackle a task is to ask that person how he or she thinks it should be tackled. Ask the person to go away and come back with suggestions which could be pursued. The reason you ask for three suggestions is that there is a stronger chance of one of the suggestions being correct or at least adaptable. When the person returns with three suggestions ask him or her to choose the suggestion that seems best. This has taken some time but it ensures that the task has not been dumped on you and that the person who had an insecurity about tackling the task has now learnt how best to tackle it.

SAYING NO GENERALLY

Remember, saying no is a way of life. It results in doing less but doing what we do well. Don't hesitate, don't give very long explanations for why you can't tackle something and certainly don't look for excuses. Perhaps sometimes you will have to offer an excuse as to why a task cannot be tackled but make sure you offer only one excuse even when there are plenty to choose from. The more excuses you offer, the weaker your case looks. When you refuse someone's request, don't apologise profusely but do keep your reply short and direct. Tell the truth: state with total honesty any limitations to what you can do or even the possibilities that you can offer. Sometimes, if you ask for time to consider a task or even ask for clarification of what the task is, you may be able to offer more constructive help or even to tackle the task itself. So don't be afraid to ask for that time or for those clarifications. But whatever you do make sure that when you say no your body language also says *no*. Make sure the inflection in your voice goes downwards on the word no and make sure that you shake your head or look concerned. Don't say no in a hesitant way which implies 'but if you twist my arm maybe I will do it anyway'.

If you can help people by doing part of what they want you to do or by doing it at a later time, say so. Explain what you can do and the limitations that you work under. If they keep on and on asking, repeat your refusal and repeat it using exactly the same reason and maybe even exactly the same language. Imagine you are pressing the action replay switch on a video recorder: just repeat the same reason. If you offer an alternative reason it looks as though you have fabricated it and you are just making excuses.

SUMMARY

Procrastination is natural. Sometimes it is justified. Sometimes it is one of the most sensible things you can do. Most of the time you should do something about it and use the tricks and tips given here to persuade yourself that tackling the task would be better than putting if off. Certainly, tackling the task would be quicker than putting it off. If you look at Exercise 5.1 you will find a game of consequences built around some of the crazier excuses you might offer. Play the game to help you get procrastination into proportion.

Fear gets in our way. It stops us working at our best and it undermines our strengths. Fear isn't always rational nor even justifiable. But whatever the reason we feel afraid, it is a very real feeling. Use the game in Exercise 5.2 to conquer your fears. After all if we talk about something and discuss it with our colleagues, that fear often disappears.

If you learn to say no you will be more helpful when you say yes. If you don't learn to say no you will not be respected or valued but your task list will be never-ending. You probably won't accomplish all the tasks and as a result you will upset the people you hoped to please. Exercise 5.3 gives you an opportunity of finding ways to say no in a number of role play situations.

EXERCISES

Exercise 5.1 – Procrastination Party

You will need:

- a supply of A4 paper
- pens or pencils
- a flipchart
- coloured flipchart pens
- time: about 30–45 minutes.

Procrastination Party is a game of consequences – a very special game of consequences because it concentrates on the reasons why we procrastinate. The best way to play it is wholeheartedly and to allow humour into the exercise. You will be building new habit paths and giving colleagues the opportunity to tease you when you tend to procrastinate; as a result they can help you out of procrastination.

Explain to the team that you are going to play a game of consequences. Issue each person with a sheet of paper and a pen or pencil, then ask one person to write on the flipchart a task over which they tend to procrastinate. Next, each person writes down an excuse for not carrying through that task and folds the piece of paper over just as in the game of consequences. Now each piece of paper is passed to the next person in a clockwise direction.

A second person writes another favourite procrastinated task on the flipchart and everyone writes down a suitable excuse and passes it around. You cannot write down the same excuse every time so as the game progresses the excuses will get wilder and more creative.

Work through the exercise until every person has had an opportunity to write a favourite procrastinated task onto the flipchart. If there are eight people in the team you will now have eight sets of excuses. Of course the excuses are jumbled up because we wrote them in the order of the suggested tasks. That doesn't matter. Open up each of the sheets of paper and ask each person to read out the reasons on their sheet as to why a task cannot be tackled. Some of the reasons will be very funny, some associated with particular tasks, others will be quite logical and serious. Use the material you now have to brainstorm why we procrastinate and how to avoid it.

Exercise 5.2 – Here be the dragons

You will need a set of fear cards (Figure 5.2) for each participant.

To make up the cards you will need plain 3 × 5 inch index cards and computer labels. Write or print one statement per label and stick the label onto the card. Make up enough sets of cards for all the participants to have their own set.

You will also need a set of dragon cards (Figure 5.3) (page 81). The dragon cards are made up in the same way as the fear cards. Once again write or print off each of the situations onto a label and stick the label onto a 3 × 5 inch index card. It is a good idea if these cards can be a different colour or written in a different colour so that it is easy to distinguish a dragon card from a fear card.

You will also need:

- a flipchart
- coloured flipchart pens
- time: about one hour.

Give each participant a complete set of fear cards. Place the dragon cards in a pile in the centre of the table. The first person to play turns over a dragon card and then selects a fear card that she believes best describes why she is afraid of that dragon. If that person is not afraid of the dragon, no fear card need be played at all.

Pass round the group until everybody has played their fear cards. Now write the name of the dragon card on the flipchart and copy down the fear card reasons. Stick that piece of flipchart paper to the wall with Blu-tak™ and ask the next person to turn up the next dragon card. Once again that person has the first opportunity of playing a fear card or of not playing a card if he is not afraid of that particular dragon. The game continues round the table until a set of fear cards is collected relating to the dragon card. Copy that dragon card and its fear cards onto a flipchart and stick that flipchart sheet to the wall.

Continue to play the game until all the dragon cards have been used or until the members of the team feel they have brought enough dragons to light.

At this stage you should have a number of completed flipcharts and now is the time for team discussion to decide how the dragons can be seen off. It is a good idea to organize a simple brainstorming session looking at each dragon; decide who was not afraid of it and ask them why they were not afraid. Their lack of fear could help the others in the team.

I'll make a fool of myself

I may make a mistake

I worry about the effect that what I do has on someone else

Any mistakes I make may affect my future prospects

I will not understand what is being said

I don't know enough about the subject

I may not be listened to

He/she will shout at me

I will have to do something I said I could do but I fear I cannot do it

I am a poor listener

I prefer to be told what to do

I hate working under pressure

People will be looking at me

I may fail

I might get into trouble

People might laugh at me

I don't know what to say

I do not understand how to do the task

My colleagues will think I'm sucking up to the boss

Other people will see my weaknesses

I may have misunderstood the instructions

I lack confidence

I hate new situations

I'm afraid of rejection

FIGURE 5.2: Fear cards

Attending a business meeting at which senior people will be present

Admitting that a task is finished and complete

Returning a phone call when a customer has called to complain

Asking people for information to help you to complete a task

Using a new computer program

Filing letters, papers and correspondence

Getting started on a new project

Telling people when they have made a mistake

Making a presentation

Writing a report on a complicated matter

Returning a call to a person known to be difficult

Doing a task that involves numbers

Proofreading for mistakes

Writing letters that say no

Explaining something to someone else

Giving criticism

Add any dragons that are particular to your business

FIGURE 5.3: Dragon cards

Exercise 5.3 – I'm sorry I can't do that

You will need:

- character sheets for each individual to be involved in the role-plays
- flipchart paper
- coloured flipchart pens
- time: about 30–45 minutes.

This exercise is about role-plays. If you have access to a camera you may wish to record the role-plays as they take place and then watch them afterwards to discuss them with the participants. If you don't have access to a camera it is best to divide people into groups of three so that two people play out the necessary roles and the third person acts as an observer.

After the role-plays are completed you will need to organize a discussion session to bring out some of the best points that have been raised. Collect those points on a flipchart so that everyone can see the good points from all the role plays, not just the ones in which they took part. The role-play sheets for role-plays 1–5 follow.

Role-play 1: Saying no to your boss

Photocopy each of these two character parts on to separate sheets of paper, obscuring the other part so that the person playing the boss does not see the individual's play-sheet and the person playing the individual does not see the boss's play-sheet.

Boss

You have just come out of a meeting with your own boss and he has reminded you that he is expecting a completed report (on a subject of your choosing) on his desk on Friday afternoon at the very latest. You had not realized the report was quite so urgent. You had actually intended to complete it but have not got very far. It was a task you began but you left for a while. The only way you can get it completed is to have a member of your staff do all the basic work for you. You realise this person is already overloaded but this task is really important. Ask the individual to complete the necessary work on the basic background of the report. It will take about five hours' work.

Individual

Your boss has a habit of dropping tasks on to you at the last minute. You think your boss is very disorganized. You have four tasks she has asked you to get done by the end of the week and you are on holiday next week. You have finished three of the tasks but you have no intention of handing them over until the last minute and you are working steadily on the fourth task. You expect it will take you about another four hours, then you will have time to tidy it up and make sure that everything is clear and organized and that your desk is ready for you to go away for a week's holiday.

You are a methodical person who likes to work things through carefully. You have just been called in for a meeting with your boss.

Role-play 2: Boss's Boss

Photocopy these two character parts on to separate sheets of paper as before.

Boss's Boss

Your immediate subordinate is someone who panics a lot. His panic is very irritating to watch so sometimes you bypass him and give tasks to his team members. When you came into the office this morning you remembered that certain information was required for the board meeting tomorrow afternoon. The information is easy enough to put together but it requires your immediate subordinate's department to produce a list of key statistics. If you ask your subordinate to organize it he will panic and rush around and your concern is that you may not get the figures on time. You decide to approach a member of his team directly and ask her to undertake the task for you. You believe it will take about two hours' work.

Individual

Your boss is a panicker. He creates panic and chaos every time he delegates a task and he never hands out tasks until the very last minute. As a result your desk is loaded with small tasks, most of which can't easily be completed because some information is lacking.

Your boss's boss, on the other hand, is very organized and efficient and you enjoy working for him. At the moment, however, you are heavily overloaded because one of your colleagues is off sick with 'flu; in addition you are one member short in the department because a colleague left last month and there is still a job vacancy. You are the calmest and most efficient member of the department and as a result your boss's boss often asks you to carry out tasks for him. Sometimes it would be better if he gave those tasks to someone else but he prefers to hand the tasks to you.

Role-play 3: Colleague

Photocopy these two character parts on to separate sheets of paper.

Team Member

You are a member of a team. Your boss has asked you to organize a team away-day. You have collected various ideas and now you need to make a decision as to whether the away-day will be:

- an outward bound session in the Lake District,
- a visit to a new computer installation,
- a group conference with exercises throughout the day culminating in a dinner.

You hate the idea of outward bound and while you don't much like the other two ideas you favour the third. You have been trying to arrange a venue but have discovered it is very difficult to select a date on which everyone can attend and for which the venues are available. You are due to go on holiday next week and if you don't sort the task out before you go away it will be too late to arrange it successfully when you get back from three weeks' holiday. This is not the only task left on your desk but it is a crucial one. You are looking for a fellow member of the team to whom you can delegate the task and your eyes light upon someone who is always very pleasant and helpful.

Individual

You feel that you are finally getting to the bottom of a loaded in-tray. You can just manage to complete two major tasks and you are well on your way to accomplishing the third. When those tasks are completed you will have a chance to review and revise, and it is your intention to reorganize your computer system and deal with a backlog of filing. You know that one of your colleagues is due to go on holiday shortly and is organizing the away-day. You have heard that there are three opportunities for the away-day and you really like the idea of going on an outward bound trip to the Lake District. You have a reputation for being helpful and you like to be involved with organizing things but this time you really don't need any extra work.

Role-play 4: Other Departments

Photocopy these two character parts on to separate sheets of paper.

The other department

You are a member of [fill in the department you prefer] and you need some crucial information from [choose a department]. You must have the information by Wednesday afternoon or you cannot complete your part of a board report. You don't know who best to ask in the [chosen department] so you have decided to go to the head of the department. You are a very efficient and organized person but you have left this request for information rather late. When you look back at your files you discover that you always seem to leave it this late and there is usually a problem.

Individual

You are the head of [fill in the name of department after discussion with your counterpart]. Your department is under a great deal of pressure at the moment because it has to produce a whole series of board papers. You have been expecting a member of [fill in the name of department after consultation with your counterpart] to call you because always, just before you have to produce your final documents for the board, they contact you and ask for some help with their papers. This time you are determined that they will get help, but the absolute minimum, and that you will bring home to them the need to do it themselves.

Role-play 5: Dumper

Photocopy these two character parts on to separate sheets of paper.

Team Member

You have just been given a task by another department. It is a task you don't like doing and you don't want to do it. Normally what you do in this situation is go to your boss who is an easy touch and ask her to explain to you how to do the task. If you look confused or worried for long enough it usually results in your boss taking over the task and doing it for you. When she hands it back to you you can just deliver it to the person who commissioned it and all is well. You are on your way to see your boss.

Boss

You are a very helpful person and you are very worried about the development and growth of your team. You want to make sure that the team members understand the tasks they tackle and that they get new experiences. You encourage them to come in and talk through their problems with you and you are very happy to stop what you are doing and explain tasks to them. One member of your team, however, seems to bring more and more tasks to you and somehow you seem to end up doing them yourself. You just see this person approaching but this time you have decided he will do the task himself, all the way through.

CHAPTER 6

Paper - Its Part In Your Downfall

KEY LEARNING POINTS

- Clutter on your desk interrupts your mind
- File to find, not to store
- Touch each piece of paper once only
- Time is another dimension of quality

INTRODUCTION

The paperless office was supposed to have come true by now . . .! We are able to scan documents into a computer and store everything in a computer file. If we don't want to do this, we can microfiche existing paper documents and store them in an easily read form. We can send E-mails and use the Internet. So why haven't we achieved the paperless office? People like paper. Computers go down. We feel safer if we can put our hands on a hard copy. Putting your hands on a hard copy is one thing – having to search through the layers on the top of your desk or delving into a pile of in-trays is a totally different matter. In this chapter you will learn how to make sure your desk is clear and ready for action every day of your working life.

To clear the desk probably means throwing away some items that are on your desk which can only be classified as rubbish. If you have out-of-date catalogues or piles of potential reading material on your desk then you have a large collection of rubbish. Many of us have other pieces of clutter on our desk ranging from the essential computer and coffee mug through to cuddly toys, dictionaries and piles of paperwork awaiting attention. Sorting the junk from the important material is the first essential step in clearing a desk and establishing a sensible filing system.

Everybody needs a filing system but the whole point of a filing system is to be able to retrieve. You do not put things into a filing system in order to store them, you put them there in order to be able to find them when you next need them. This revolutionary thought should change the way that you design your filing. Alphabetical filing may not always be the best. In this chapter we look at a simple filing system that works and helps you keep your desk clear.

Time is another dimension of quality. How long do pieces of paper spend lounging around in in-trays in your organization? How long does it take a vital document to travel between two departments? What happens to documents when they leave one department and journey on to another? If you don't know the answer to these and many more questions you don't have a dimension of quality being added in the form of time. In this chapter we look at how we can enhance that dimension of quality. The exercises at the end of this chapter concentrate on ways of helping you minimize the paper and maximize your efficiency.

HOW TO CLEAR YOUR DESK AND KEEP IT CLEAR

When I say 'desk' we need to think about your desk and all the clutter on it together with your in-tray. A lot of organizations that I know have a clear desk policy. A clear desk policy makes complete sense in today's world.

Scenario — Secure information

Once upon a time, in the days before clear desk policies, a leading firm of professional advisors had a break-in overnight. When everyone arrived the next day it was obvious that the organization had been broken into but strangely enough nothing seemed to be missing. The safe was intact. The petty cash box was where it had always been and contained what it had always contained. Nobody reported anything of value stolen from their desks or their desk drawers. And then one individual spotted that a pile of papers seemed to be in a slightly different order. Sure enough, within half an hour a key piece of information relevant to a client of the business was available for public knowledge. That piece of information seriously affected the client's flotation on the Stock Exchange and caused many repercussions.

Yes, that was a large organization and the information concerned related to a public quoted company but everyone has information on their desk that others would like to own. What do your competitors want to know about you? What do your staff want to know about you? Locking away information at night simply makes the organization more secure.

Scenario — Soggy information

One day I walked into a client organization and was fascinated to find strings tied across the office just above head height. Pinned to the strings with a series of pegs or balanced across them were pieces of paperwork and files. The whole office looked like some crazy scene out of a washing-day movie. What was going on? And then I spotted one or two people with hairdryers who seemed to be applying the draught from the hairdryer to the paper strung across the office. Others were working with rulers but several people were sitting at their desks working normally. The carpet seemed squelchy. And the story goes like this.

On their way out the night before someone had stubbed out a cigarette and left it in an ashtray. Unfortunately the cigarette had not gone out completely and when the ashtray was tipped into the wastepaper basket as a final gesture before leaving the office, the ashtray contained a smouldering cigarette. That smouldering cigarette gradually ignited a piece of paper and the piece of paper caused a fire in the wastepaper basket. The fire caused the sprinkler system to start. If it rains in your office and you have paper on your desk that paper is likely to turn into papier-maché.

What I saw was the aftermath of a rain-shower in an office. Those who had left the papers on their desks were trying to separate them and dry them out. Those who had put their papers away were smugly getting on with their tasks.

If that doesn't convince you maybe £750,000 will.

Scenario – Misplaced information

It was a cheque for £750,000 and it arrived in the accounts department late on a Friday afternoon. Too late to bank it and as a result it did not get attended to. The man on whose desk it arrived was not a tidy worker but he did like to clear up his papers at night. So when it came to the end of the day he shuffled all his papers together and thrust them into a desk drawer. He forgot all about the cheque. On Monday morning he returned to the office, took his pile of papers out and commenced work. It was not until Monday afternoon that he thought about the cheque. He looked through the pile of papers. The cheque was not there. 'Not to worry,' he assumed, 'the cheque is probably with my boss.' By Tuesday morning he became more concerned about the whereabouts of the cheque and checked with his boss. No, his boss had not seen the cheque. Together they returned to the desk and searched through every piece of paper but the cheque was not there. Eventually the disappearance of the cheque had to be reported but not before the managing director had hit a problem with the bank. This was a simple problem, easily solved: all they had to do was to ask the customer to provide them with a second cheque. The jokes rolling around the office were plentiful. Anyone who went sick was deemed to have left for the Bahamas with a cheque for £750,000.

The story doesn't end there: Shortly after the incident it was time for the office Christmas party and the man on whose desk the cheque had landed looked through his pile of papers to find the office Christmas party invitation memo. It was two pages long and the two pages were held together with a paper clip, and in between the two pages was a cheque for £750,000.

Paper clips are greedy things: if they can find something else and take that something into their grasp they will do so. Just sweeping papers off a desk and thrusting them into a drawer at night might be adhering to the clear desk policy but it certainly does not make sure that a desk is organized and paperwork accessible.

If none of these reasons have convinced you that you need a clear desk, then just think how much easier it will be to start work if every morning you came into the first day of the next part of your life. Those who meet a pile of paperwork on their desk are meeting the leftover problems of yesterday; those who come to a clean desk come to the start of the future.

There is only one way to clear a desk and that is to take everything that is on the desk off the desk and start from there. Pile up all the paperwork and files into one big pile – or several big piles if your desk is particularly badly cluttered. Next, begin with the files. Make a list of which files they are and why they are on your desk. For example, are you working on them, waiting for something to happen or are they simply there waiting to be filed? Once you have your list put the pile of files out of sight. Preferably put the pile of files away in the filing system but if your filing system doesn't work that way you will have to wait until we get to a later section of this chapter.

Now you need to sort through the piles on the desk. They are likely to fall into four categories:

- *Action piles* These are the pieces of paper, documents or even files that are on your desk because you need to work on them.
- *Information piles* These are the pieces of paper or files that are on your desk because you are waiting for someone else to give you information so that you can work on them.
- *Reading piles* These are the piles of documents or pieces of paper that are on your desk because you think you ought to read them.
- *Rubbish piles* These are the items that are on your desk because they seem too important, too good or too interesting to throw away. However, you have no intention of dealing with them and you are never likely to use them again.

There may be a fifth pile and that is the pile that should have been filed but hasn't been filed. Very often the fifth pile is in an in-tray or it may be on the desk simply because you are not sure how to get it off the desk.

Begin by sorting everything that remains on your desk into action, information, reading, rubbish, filing. All you should be left with is your computer, your telephone and perhaps your coffee mug. There should be nothing else on your desk. Many desks that I see would now be stripped down to a level of pens, books, cuddly toys, photographs and other clutter. If the desk is to be a clear working zone, it is a good idea to get all these pieces of clutter off the desk too. Do you really need the cuddly toy? Can you put the reference books out of sight on a shelf? After all, reference books are in themselves a distraction – you only need them to refer to when you seek that reference. Try getting a shelf put up somewhere near your desk for reference books. If that is entirely impossible try at least to get them out of sight in a cupboard. Working at my desk I have a cupboard over the top of the desk which contains all the reference books behind glass. This clears them out of sight and out of mind.

Do you really need pots of pens and pencils on your desk? Do you really need all those little Post-it™ notes and the collection of other bits and pieces? If you do, fine, but the majority of us don't and those things are better put in a desk drawer out of sight and tidied away.

THE ACTION PILE

Now your desk is completely clear there is space to put the action pile back on it. But you haven't finished with it. You can't take action on everything at once and some of the action should not be taken by you. So your first activity is to go through your action pile and sort it.

- Put it into a pile of tasks that you have to do and prioritize those tasks with deadlines.
- Create a second pile of tasks that someone else has to do; in other words, the pieces of paper that have to be handed on.
- Next, make a note of what action has to be taken: is it a phone call, a letter, a meeting or a piece of work?

Now turn to the various piles. If there is a pile that should be passed on to someone else, write a comment on it and immediately pass it on. Don't hold on to paperwork that someone else is waiting for. If it needs more of an explanation than simply being passed on, make sure that you have made a date to talk to the individual

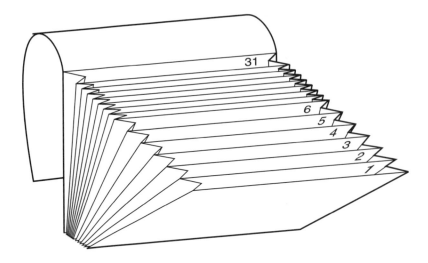

Figure 6.1: Day-numbered elephant file

concerned about the paperwork and that you are ready to pass it on when necessary. All that is left now is the action pile, prioritized by deadline. To simplify working with your action pile you need an elephant file.

To be truthful, you need two elephant files if you have a very busy diary. The first elephant file should be numbered 1 to 31 (Figure 6.1) and the second one dated with the months of the year. Take your diary and mark into your diary the tasks that need to be accomplished and the days on which you will work on them. Plan your diary carefully, remembering the lessons of Chapter 4, and make sure that you don't allocate too much work to one day. When you have allocated a piece of work to one day put it into the same numbered slot in your elephant file. For example you have a report to write that has to be completed by the 18th and you decide to plan it into the 14th. Take all the paperwork relating to that report and put it into the slot labelled the 14th in your elephant file. When you have completed this task all the action paperwork will be safely in the elephant file and recorded in your diary. Now you can tie up the elephant file and put it in your desk.

You might need a 12-month elephant file if you are somebody who plans a long way ahead. As a trainer running workshops I run both a daily and a monthly elephant file. The current month's papers are all in the numbered file and the up-and-coming bookings are in the month-dated file. As soon as one file begins to be emptied and you are halfway through the month the paperwork from the next month is inserted into the daily-numbered file.

THE INFORMATION PILE

With all the action paper off the desk you are now left with those tricky pieces of paper which are waiting for information from someone else. First we need a set of rules here. If you need information by 19 March you should certainly not leave it until 19 or 20 March to chase up the information that hasn't arrived. Nor should you leave it in your own mind that you need it by 19 March and expect the other person to guess that fact. No, your trick is to put the information pile into the same elephant file that you used for the action pile. But you are not going to put it into the day that you require the information: put it into the day before you require the information and that will remind you to chase the relevant individual one day before the information is due. If they have read this book and worked through the exercises they will have prioritized anyway and your friendly reminder will only serve to confirm that the paperwork is on its way. If, however, they haven't read this book you will probably force an urgent prioritization on them and they will grab your piece of paperwork from the bottom of the pile on their desk and start to work on it. Either way you are likely to get your paperwork and information back on time.

Whenever you put something into your elephant file you will of course make a note in your diary so that you can double-check and find it again. All that you need to do now is to make sure that every morning you open the elephant file and take out the relevant pieces of paperwork to work on them.

THE READING PILE

Are you really going to read it? Do you feel you ought to read it? Is there a pile of magazines or relevant documents to your business that are mounting up month by month? Are you at the head of a reader list and does the magazine stop with you? If you are going to answer yes to any of these questions then you need to deal very drastically with your reading pile. We have a rule in our organization: if something has not been read within six working days then it is unlikely to be read at all. Decide your time limit for reading and give your reading pile a life. Stamp it with the date it arrives and make sure that when the six days are up you get rid of it. Getting rid of it may be passing it on to the next person on the list or it may simply be putting it into the wastepaper basket because you have no intention of reading it.

An alternative to dealing with the reading pile is to delegate it. Many years ago, when I was partner in a firm of accountants, I was faced with volumes of reading – volumes of magazines and information that I really ought to have read but for which I had very little time. However, I did have a number of junior staff. It was a simple matter to allocate a magazine to other members of staff and ask them to read it on my behalf. All I did was to read the contents page marking with a highlighter pen the articles that I was particularly interested in and the person reading the magazine for me had the duty of reading those articles and writing me a one-page précis. The précis had to take the format of bullet points. Of course it didn't mean they only read that chapter or page of the magazine – they had to read the whole of the magazine to give me any highlights that I might have missed. And yes, there was groaning and moaning in the land, but suddenly people who were given reading duties realized they weren't just doing my reading for me, they were getting additional information and it was enabling them to pass their exams. Is there anyone in your organization who could do the reading for you?

If you work in a department in which several people receive the same reading matter, can you take it in turns to read it and produce a précis bullet-point sheet? But whatever you do, don't leave wobbly piles of reading on your desk with good intentions. Throw them away or pass them on if you have no real intention of reading them.

THE RUBBISH PILE

The rubbish pile is a tragic pile. It is full of things that you feel one day might be useful but you can't think where to put them. It has things in it that seem too good to throw away – catalogues from an exhibition or clippings from a magazine of a once-interesting article that you can't now really find a use for. These items are rubbish. They belong in the wastepaper basket and they should not come out until the wastepaper basket is emptied. Be drastic. If you are a natural hoarder your instinct will be to keep far too much. If you are really unsure, set up two levels of wastepaper basket:

- the wastepaper basket that takes pure rubbish and is thrown away, and
- the wastepaper basket that takes things that you believe might be rubbish but which will not be thrown away for another month.

Once a month that basket has to be emptied and all the things in it that are over a month old are thrown away. After all, if you haven't gone through the pile to look for the items that were in the one-month delay rubbish then you certainly don't need them.

If you have gone through the four piles you have probably cleared your desk with the exception of the filing (and that is covered in the next section) and next you need to decide what *should* be on your desk. Make sure your desk is equipped for action. Is your telephone to hand and does it have easy access to a notepad? Can you see your computer screen and type without risk to yourself on your keyboard? Have you got enough light to work or do you need a light fixed to your desk? In clearing your desk you are clearing it for action, not to put on a display, so make sure that as much of the desk is as bare as possible. Make sure your desk is big enough for the tasks you need to do on it but do remember that clutter takes up more space then necessary. If you need readily accessed information, can you put it into chart format and put it on the wall above your desk? Have you turned out the drawers of your desk? Throw away all the broken pencil stubs and bits of paper that seemed as though they might be useful one day. Are the desk drawers stacked with the things that you put in there because there didn't seem to be anywhere else to put them? Keep only the things in your desk that you will genuinely use and need. Make a note in your diary to have a regular turn-out of your desk drawers so that they don't build up to the fluff level again.

Next, take a look at the area surrounding your desk and make sure that anything you need access to is within easy grasp. For example, the wastepaper basket should be near enough to tempt you to use it. If you set up a system that requires the delayed wastepaper basked then make absolutely sure that is also within easy reach. Make sure your in-tray is within reach but preferably behind you so that it cannot distract you too easily. Of course, you are going to empty it as soon as things come into it and you are going to handle each item once, distributing it onwards. That is a very simple rule: *touch each piece of paper once*. If you can possibly do this you will be making sure that nothing sits on your desk waiting for you to do something with it or pass it on to someone else. As your daily delivery of mail arrives at your desk, go through it:

- throw away the rubbish
- put the filing into the filing system
- put the action and information pieces into your elephant file and mark your diary
- put the reading into the action day on which you will read it – and
- throw away the rubbish.

It will take only a few moments at the time of your incoming mail arriving but it will take a very long time if you let it build up for a few weeks.

A SIMPLE FILING SYSTEM WORKS BEST

Try to make sure that only one person in the department keeps a copy of paperwork. If at all possible, departments should have a reliable and easily accessible central filing system. If you are tempted to keep duplicate papers in your own system you will only cause confusion, so try not to do so. Your first step should be to make sure that the central filing system works for you. There are things, of course, that we do need to keep in our own personal filing system and now you need to consider those.

Do you have a filing system? I ask the question because many people don't. Many people have a filing cabinet into which they stuff things or even a briefcase where ancillary piles are put. Some people simply have piles on their desk. The most common reason I am given for not filing something is because *once filed it will never be found again*. If that is your reason for not filing documents and pieces of paper then there is something wrong with your filing system. What goes wrong with most filing systems is that documents are put into the system in order to store them but not necessarily in order to retrieve them. The whole point of a filing system is to be able to gain access to something that is stored there.

Once you have cleared your desk you will have a pile of documents that need filing. Before we turn to the filing system you need to clear your briefcase. Is there a permafrost level in your briefcase? The permafrost level is the level below which your fingers do not go. Many a briefcase has been opened in front of me on a workshop only to find a level below which the fingers do not attempt to wander. That level is often designated by a pile of old newspapers or perhaps a divider within the briefcase. Below that level lie the things that are never disturbed. When we do disturb the layer of permafrost, we usually find a few things that we had forgotten were there. One participant on a workshop found his passport, a pile of family photographs and something rather nasty and sticky that had possibly once been a sweet. Someone else found a missing pair of hair curlers and I have to admit that I once found a jar of pickle in the bottom of a handbag! These are all things that descend below the permafrost level and stay there if you do not turn out the briefcase. So having cleared your desk your next job is to empty your briefcase and check out the contents that lie there. Briefcases are necessary to carry work and personal items to and from the office. This means they only carry work if you are going to work on it or if you are going to a meeting. There is very little point in taking papers home if you have no intention of working on them. The briefcase is certainly not an ancillary file nor somewhere to store documents. Anything that is in your briefcase should be going to be used within the next 24 hours. This means that if you don't intend to re-read the old newspaper you should throw it away. Better still, leave it on the train or bus or put it into some kind of wastepaper basket on your journey to work so that you don't even have to carry it very far.

What else is in your briefcase? Treat it like your desk and throw away all the rubbish, put the action material and the waiting-for-information material into your elephant file system. Now take out those items of reading that have travelled for a long while and check them out. Did they arrive more than six days ago?, in which case put them into the wastepaper basket. Do they still have a genuine reading life and do you intend to read them? If so, put them into your elephant file on the relevant day you plan to read them. If your journey involves travelling on public transport then you may well wish to put them into your briefcase tonight and take them home to read on your journey.

Next, check out the everyday essentials that belong in your briefcase. Do you carry headache pills? Do you carry an umbrella? Do you carry essential items such as marker pens, Post-it™ notes, a book for taking notes at meetings? Each of us has essential supplies that must travel with us all the time. Make sure these are replenished and in working order. It is a good idea to give your briefcase a domicile: either it lives at home, in which case every time it goes home you check it out and make sure everything you need is in there and nothing that you don't need is in there, or it has a domicile at work and the same checking takes place each morning.

Out of your briefcase will probably have come some further documents for filing. Add them to the pile.

Before you start to file, turn to your filing cabinet and look at it. Try to look at it with new eyes and see it as a valuable source of information. Begin by checking out this filing cabinet to make sure that it doesn't contain unnecessary paperwork at present. I once knew a marketing department of an organization that simply bought a new filing cabinet every time they ran out of space. Eventually, of course, they ran out of office space and finally they ran out of building space. They had a lot of filing cabinets, most of which were never opened, and those that were opened had so many documents in them that the important ones were buried behind the unimportant.

Your first task on your filing cabinet is to weed it. Does it contain anything that is out of date, no longer required or obsolete? There may be things in there that could go into long-term storage – such as dead files that are needed for legal requirements but are not needed to work on. Remove any dead files from your filing cabinet.

Next, are there any files that are not required for legal purposes but are dead and will never be opened again? Put these files into the wastepaper basket. If this makes you afraid put them into your delay wastepaper basket and see whether you refer to them within one month. If you don't refer to them in that period, then throw them away.

Now turn to the active files, the ones that need to remain in your filing cabinet, and check them out too. A very fat file containing lots of pieces of paper is a difficult place to find information. A series of smaller, thin files is much easier to check through. Should you divide the correspondence into various sections? Remember the information in the file is there to work for you not to be a hurdle across which you have to climb. Are there any duplicate papers on the file? This happens very easily: first we file the original file note and then we file the secondary file note with something else scribbled on it. When that happens you need to take off the original file note to minimize the paper. If a file has become very large and very difficult to work through, why not consign it to the dead or limbo file section and open up a fresh one for that particular client or subject? Your limbo section could be a filing cabinet which contains material you may refer to for the next six months but which ultimately will pass into the dead section as new papers and fresher subjects arrive. The Pareto principle says that 80 per cent of the material that arrives on our desk is junk. It follows that 80 per cent of the contents of our filing cabinets are junk too. If in your weeding you are fairly drastic and take as much as 50 per cent of the material out of your filing cabinet, you will find you still have substantial amounts of documents that you will never use again.

Once you have completed your first task of weeding the filing cabinet and the individual files in the filing cabinet, you are now ready to ask yourself whether the system that you have actually works for you. There is only one question to ask: can you find what you are looking for? If your answer is yes then your system works exactly for you and all you need to do now is file away the items that are waiting on your desk. If your system doesn't work for you and your answer is no, you now need to think very seriously about the kind of filing system you should have. The dangers in a filing system are that information is not quickly and easily recognizable and available. The easiest way to make information quickly recognizable and available is to use some kind of colour coding. Try to obtain a series of coloured files and make sure that you code different types of information with different colours. For example, if you have to work on financial matters you might choose to code these with red files; projects might be green, staff matters blue, reference in the form of catalogues, yellow. The colour system is entirely up to you, but if you do colour-code your filing system you will find it a lot easier to put your hands on things quickly.

The next key suggestion is to make sure that you have a large number of small files rather than a small number of large files. That means it is better to have lots of categories than one big category.

My biggest dread when I look at someone's filing system is the alphabetical-order system for enquiries. This means that you have to remember the name of the company or the person who raised the enquiry or you have to keep going through the alphabetical system. It also means that you have to decide whether Jane Allan Associates is filed under J for *Jane* Allan and Associates or A for Jane *Allan* and Associates. An enquiry system would be far better filed under the subject matter of the enquiry, cross-referenced alphabetically. All you are trying to do is to make sure the retrieval is ready for the reason you need to retrieve.

Having colour-coded your files you will probably need now to activity-code them. The files that you refer to every day should be in the easiest and most accessible drawers of the filing cabinet. The files that you only refer to occasionally should be in the less accessible drawers. And the files that you are never going to refer to again should have gone into the dead filing section.

Now we have colour-coded the activity-rated files. How are you going to file the information? By subject category? Alphabetically? Date order? Numerically? The decision must be yours. But you should bear in mind a number of key thoughts:

- People remember names and not numbers, so the numerical filing system needs always to have some kind of index.
- People don't necessarily think of the name of the person they contacted but they do think of the subject matter, so an alphabetical system also needs to be cross-filed under subject matter.
- The date may be important when deadlines are occurring but it is very rarely remembered a long time after the incident. Anything filed specifically by date order would need to have some kind of cross-referencing system.

It looks like we have gone for a subject category. Within the subject matter you will probably want to decide whether to file by date or alphabetical order. Date is probably better as long as the date is clearly visible on the piece of paper and you can access it quickly. Once you have decided on the categories and classification type in your filing system all that remains is to move your files around until they work. If they don't work and things don't fit, and if, after a trial period of a week to ten days you can't find what you want, there is something wrong with your new system and you should sit down and work it out again. Remember, your main aim is to be able to find things and not to store them.

SUMMARY

In this chapter we have looked at paper and its part in your downfall. Paper stored or collected around your work area can turn itself into a barrier to prevent work taking place. First, you need to clear your desk. Make sure that the essential things are available on your desk easily and that other things are to hand but at the same time make sure that your desk does not become a storage spot for paper. Next, you need to clear your filing cabinet, not forgetting to check out the briefcase as you go. Make sure that the filing cabinet is not full of paper that is preventing you from finding the paper that you need. The following exercises give you the opportunity to practise the skills covered by this chapter.

EXERCISES

Exercise 6.1 – Clear that desk

You will need:

- flipchart paper
- desk category sheets (Figure 6.2)
- A4 paper
- flipchart pens
- time: about two hours for preparation and 30–45 minutes for discussion.

The purpose of this exercise is to get everybody in the team to examine the contents of their desk and decide into which categories they fall. Allow everyone plenty of time to go through their desks and make a list of the paperwork falling into:

- action piles
- information piles
- reading piles
- rubbish piles
- filing piles

Don't ask them to do anything with it yet; just ask them to bring their completed sheets to a meeting. Then organize a discussion as to how people can work better and set up their own action files. Your aim is to have the team brainstorm and come up with better ways of keeping information and of making sure that information is accessible. When it comes to filing, you may well want to discuss how a central filing system could work and to collect the general views. It is a good idea to prepare a flipchart sheet with each of the key headings and encourage people to put their views and ideas down so that a consistent approach can be taken throughout the department.

	What to do!
Action	
Information	
Reading	
Rubbish	
Filing	

FIGURE 6.2: Desk categories sheet

Exercise 6.2 – The clutter swamp

To make this exercise very relevant indeed you will need to do some careful background work. Either first thing in the morning or last thing in the evening, when most people have gone home, spend some time going through the contents of two or three people's desks. Make a list of the typical items that land on those desks, then write each item onto a card. Make up three or four sets of cards of items that could be found on the desks in your organization.

Now you will need:

- flipchart paper
- coloured flipchart pens
- a supply of dilemma sheets (Figure 6.3) copied onto A4 paper for each participant
- the supply of cards that you have prepared with typical items that land on the desks
- time: about one hour.

Break the teams up into groups of two or three and deal out the sets of cards. Ask each group to pick up one card and then fill in individually a dilemma sheet. They should write the problem in the middle box and then describe four options as to what could happen to that document; in the outer boxes they should write their reasons for their actions. Allow everybody about five minutes to prepare an individual dilemma sheet per card. Then, in their small group discussions, ask them to come up with a preferred option and its reasons. Allow about 20 minutes for this exercise.

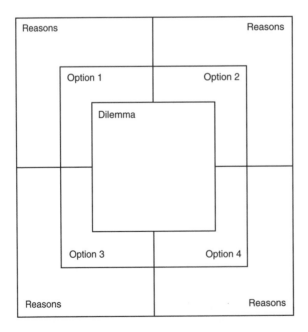

FIGURE 6.3: Dilemma sheet

Next, take each problem one by one; head it up on a flipchart and lead a discussion with the whole team deciding how best to get various items off desks.

CHAPTER 7

COMMUNICATION

KEY LEARNING POINTS
- People read white space
- Match your message to the receiver
- Plan your phone calls
- Make it easier for people to do what you want

INTRODUCTION

While it might be rather glib to blame communication for all the ills in any business, communication frequently lies at the heart of many problems. Poor communication results in wasted time and inefficient communication uses too much time. Communication is simply the transference of a thought or idea between one person and another. If you think of one individual as the transmitter and the other as the receiver, all you have to do is to ensure that message travels between the two in the most effective way. This chapter looks very specifically at writing letters, memos and faxes with time in mind. It will show you how to write each of these documents for impact. Included too is a way of 'fog testing' your writing so that you can be satisfied that someone else will have the best possible chance of understanding it.

Perhaps one of the biggest time-wasters is the telephone. Because you cannot know what the other person is doing when you pick up your phone and make a call, the phone will always be an interruption to that person. We are all aware of this and as a result we tend to be more polite and slower to get to the point when talking on the telephone. If you are on the receiving end of a phone call, despite it being an interruption, there is a sense of urgency from a ringing phone that makes us answer it. Indeed, in many organizations there is a three-ring rule: you must answer the phone within three rings, which means that whatever time your caller chooses to contact you, you will have to leap to respond. Without destroying the quality level of the three-ring rule this chapter will show you how to make a quiet hour plan.

An essential element of communication is the art of listening. Most of us are very poor at listening: too busy thinking our own thoughts, making up the reply that we will give when the speaker has finished or even drifting away. This part of the chapter will show you how to analyse the way you listen and the way others listen to make sure that you speak and listen on the same wavelength. It also includes tips for maximizing the information you get from the listening exercise.

HOW TO WRITE LETTERS, MEMOS AND FAXES THAT GET READ

What stops people reading the documents that cross their desks is the way those documents look. Have a look at the four documents illustrated in Figure 7.1. Each of them has arrived on your desk at the same time and each of them is from someone equally important and is on an equally vital subject. Sadly you have only got time to read one of the documents. The question I ask everybody when they attend a time management or even a communication skills workshop is: *Which document would you read first*?

Perhaps it doesn't surprise you to learn that over 95 per cent of the people asked always say they would read document C first. Document B comes next but the majority of people say they would never ever get round to reading document D. So why do we write them? The only reason I ask these questions is because documents D do exist. They are written long because people think it is quicker just to dictate material from the top of their heads and then to sign it afterwards. People who write document C think about what they have to say first and plan the impact. This section of the chapter is about planning impact.

There are some very simple rules that apply to writing letters. These rules cover:

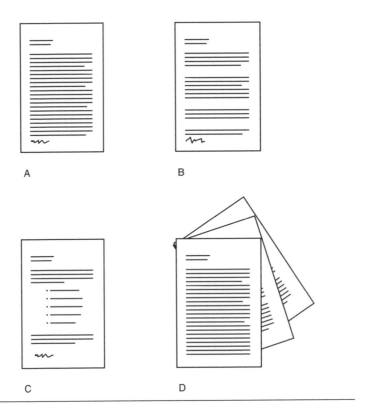

FIGURE 7.1: Four different document layouts

- layout
- vocabulary
- sentences
- punctuation

If you apply the simple rules at all times your writing will have a level of impact that ensures firstly that it gets read and secondly that its message is understood. But remember that to do this well you will always have to plan what you are going to write.

Many years ago I worked as a journalist. We were taught that if we needed to produce 1000 words then we should write 2000 words and then cut our material back to 1000. If you do this you will write in a tight and economic way. No superfluous material is included. No repetition. Some people write a bare 1000 words and leave all the padding in. Other people write 848 words and then add other words to pad out what they have to say. When you read a piece of published writing you can tell the difference. You can easily spot the piece that was written long and cut short: it is more interesting to read. What you can really see is the planning that lies behind it. Make sure that planning always lies behind your letters, memos and faxes and they will work.

LAYOUT

With the advent of the word processor came the bullet point. A bullet point is really a full stop used before part of a sentence rather than at the end of it. Now the purpose of the full stop is simply to tell you that a thought has ended and something new is beginning. By putting the full stop before the thought you are alerting someone's attention to something new and exciting. It is almost like screaming *Listen now!* when you speak. The best layouts use bullet points for key items that must not be missed.

People read white space. When you looked at Figure 7.1 and chose the document labelled C, you chose white space. You chose it probably because it looked as though the writer had organized his or her thoughts by bullet pointing and displaying them on the page. But, quite frankly, what you were opting for was to read white space. It looks less like hard work. The way you create white space on the page is to design your layout. A good tip is always to shrink your piece of writing to thumbnail sketch on the computer and look at the impact on the page. Is there a shape? Does it look as if it could be read reasonably swiftly? A good layout will have shape on the page and will make sure there is white space. One way to ensure white space is using bullet points. Another way is to paragraph.

A paragraph is a collection of sentences on the same subject. However, you need to decide what the subject matter is. You could write a letter that comprises one long paragraph because the subject of the letter is all the same. Or you could take that same letter and divide it into several paragraphs. Sometimes I suggest to writers that they should artificially paragraph their letters: that is, to create a paragraph where they might otherwise be tempted not to. They do it because the impact of the paragraph is very strong.

VOCABULARY

The size of our vocabulary is really the story of our lives to date. If you were an avid reader as a child your vocabulary will have expanded far faster than the person who was fascinated by mathematics. If you are a crossword-puzzle enthusiast your vocabulary will not only be large but to some extent it will be obscure. After all, how often do we use the word ling to mean heather? Crossword puzzlers use it all the time, of course. Many professions have their own vocabulary. We might refer to account-speak, IT-speak, engineer-speak, marketing-speak; we will be talking about language in its abbreviated or jargon form which is sometimes used as a barrier against outsiders. The value of the various jargon speaks is that they can save time when one professional speaks to another. The problem with the various jargon speaks is that they do create barriers to external communication.

When you read a novel you probably read for enjoyment and maybe even to savour the way the novel is written. When you read a piece of business writing you read it to get information as quickly as possible. So in business writing stick to short and simple words that everyone understands. Simple words will never get in the way. They are most likely to be fully understood by anyone and they will create an effortless read. I find that simple words also have more energy. Just think about the following:

- I will attempt to do that.
- I will try to do that.

The second sentence actually sounds as though the writer might make an effort. The first sentence, while it has a very similar meaning, does not make the same energized impression.

If you have to use jargon words make sure that your jargon itself is not surrounded by longer everyday words. Use only jargon when you are satisfied that the communication is taking place between two people who have access to exactly the same level of jargon.

SENTENCES

A sentence is a unit of information. The longer the unit the more confusing. If you read a long sentence you very often have to go back to the beginning of the sentence more than once in order to check out exactly what you are reading about. That consumes time and might even waste time. But perhaps more dangerously, the longer the sentence the greater the possibility for misinterpretation, misunderstanding or skip-reading. When faced with long sentences a lot of people read the opening words of the sentence and then skip past the middle content to the end of the sentence. After all, the sentence itself looks daunting and this is a quick way to assimilate the information.

In order to get your sentences read, write them short. Write them in the active voice too. Quite a lot of people seem to have access to two styles of communication: their spoken style which is natural and their written style which becomes heavier, more pompous and is built around long and complicated words. Sometimes we even write our letters in the passive tense.

It is easy to spot the passive: that which is being done comes first in the sentence followed by part of the verb to be and followed by the person doing the action.

The book is read by Mary.

is a passive sentence as a way of saying:

Mary is reading a book.

Of course a passive gives an additional opportunity and that is simply to say:

The book is read.

This gives no indication as to who is reading it and allows total anonymity. But when you read it do you feel anonymity or do you feel that someone is washing their hands of the subject matter? I believe the passive tense makes us feel that people are not interested in the subject nor in the reader. What is more, it is confusing and can be misinterpreted. A lot of time is wasted on communication that is misinterpreted. So write in simple active sentences using direct verbs.

PUNCTUATION

If your business letters are to be kept short, succinct and to the point they will need the minimum of punctuation.

- *A full stop* Tells you when a sentence has been finished.
- *A colon* Tells you that a list of items is to follow. I believe its best use in business writing is to warn that a list of bullet points is about to follow. Of course you could use it to connect together two sentences which have a similar theme. The resulting sentence would be rather long and confusing.
- *A comma* Allows a breathing space. But don't be tempted to use them like brackets. Sometimes in correspondence thoughts can seem to be bracketed off by commas rather than the commas being used to give breathing space in a longer sentence.

You will have noticed in the list above I have missed out the semi-colon. I don't believe it has a place in business writing, certainly not in time-orientated writing. There are several reasons for this:

- It creates longer sentences.
- Its use is not always understood.
- It lacks the dramatic impact of the bullet point.

Remember the purpose of your punctuation is to emphasize meaning and to clarify. Punctuation should not be a hurdle over which the reader has to climb. Once you have written your letter, memo or fax you need to be certain that it will be understood by your reader. A good way of checking out the readability of what you have written is to apply a **fog test**. Your computer software may even include a fog test in its options. However the simplest and easiest fog tests can be done manually just as quickly.

FOG TESTING

To test for the fogginess of a letter, memo or fax:

1. Go through your piece of writing and count up the number of sentences. This is one element to your fog score.
2. Next read through the writing again and this time count up the number of words that have more than two syllables. Words of more than two syllables can be counted as long words in the English language.
3. Next take your total of long words and divide them by the number of sentences. The result is a fog factor.

The fog factor

- 2/3   Factors of two or three produce a reasonable letter which will be read very swiftly by any reader.
- 4/5   Factors of four to five probably include too many long words but if the letter is on a technical subject and addressed to someone who speaks the same technical language the letter will be fine.
- 6+   A factor of six or more will result in a very difficult letter. This is a letter that will have too many long words and too few sentences. If the layout is unattractive too this is a letter that will not be read.

If you read through your letter and discover that it has a fog score that is too high, consider the following:

- Omit any unnecessary words.
- Replace long words with shorter words.
- Divide up your long sentences into two or three shorter ones.

THE PRAT RULE

So what makes written communication maximize the use of time?

- It must look interesting.
- It must be as short as possible without loss of content.

- The meaning must be clear and must come across aided by the punctuation.
- The words used in the communication must be as simple and straightforward as possible.
- Finally, the communication should carry authority. It should tell the readers exactly what will happen next and what they have to do.

So when you plan your letter you will probably want to use the following grid:

- The **P**resent   A description of a situation as it stands – the reason for writing.
- The **R**eason for writing   We don't write about a situation, we write about what has happened as a result of the situation which is perhaps creating confusion.
- The **A**ction that must be taken   What the reader should do as a result of having read the letter.
- **T**hanks   A simple politeness to indicate that you are grateful that the reader has spent time reading the letter.

Put together it spells **Prat**! If you design your letters around **Prat** you will make sure that the reader begins by discovering the subject of the letter and then learns about any complications to the situation, next logically finding out what he or she must do. If the letter finishes with a verbal handshake, the reader feels pleasantly rewarded for reading it. Now you have a fog-proof, well-written and well-designed piece of communication. And that is what gets read.

THE QUIET HOUR CONCEPT

Just imagine that the telephone on your desk did not ring for one whole hour. Just imagine that hour was at your busiest point of the day – and at a point when you can achieve most. Would you get three hours' work done? Most people estimate that if they had one hour's peace and quiet from a ringing telephone when their brains were at their peak they could achieve three times as much work as they might normally do otherwise.

So why don't we do it? Well, anyone making a phone call to us cannot possibly know when we have chosen our quiet hour unless we tell them. The first trick in working with the telephone and controlling time is to tell people the best time of day to make calls to you. Obviously this is far more easily done within the organization than externally, but it is still possible to control external phone calls.

The way you do it is quite simple: you tell people when is the best time for them to get hold of you. Very few people choose to ring outside the best possible time. What of course you have done is minimized interruptions during the period that was not labelled the best possible time. Of course, you have to be flexible and you have to keep your job and its duties in mind. If you are a help desk, making the best possible time to be only one hour at the end of the day would not be very supportive. But there is no doubt that you could have the best possible sections of an hour or maybe even a rota for the best possible times for contacting each individual on the help desk.

Naturally, setting up the best possible time concept won't clear you of all incoming phone calls. Now we need a second plan. Plan B involves an answerphone, voice mail or that very simple device – a colleague. Under plan B you arrange one hour during your peak performance time when you will not accept telephone calls. This doesn't mean your telephone won't be answered, it means it will be answered by some other device or individual. Perhaps it will be answered by your personal answerphone on your desk. Perhaps your telephone will be switched to voice mail. Perhaps your telephone will be answered by a colleague who has volunteered to answer during your quiet hour because you volunteered to answer during his or her quiet hour. Whatever you do, the actual quiet hour process will also become an education process. I made this suggestion in a client's company many years ago. And this is the story of their experience.

Scenario – A quiet hour

Managers backed each other up. Imagine that Susan is now backed up by Bill. During Susan's quiet hour Bill would answer not only his own telephone but also Susan's phone. During the first weeks of the experiment Bill took a number of messages and calls for Susan. He handed over the notes and an efficient service ensued. After a while, however, the calls started to dry up. People had begun to realize that if you rang Susan at that particular time you always got Bill. 'I won't ring her now, I will wait until she is back at her desk,' was the conclusion. Remember that you can only take calls for a colleague for a very short period of time or you will end up taking only exception calls.

Outside your quiet hour time you will be taking and making phone calls. This means you will be vulnerable to the amount of time that is wasted during a phone conversation. Most phone conversations waste time because the two parties to the conversation have not planned what they have to say. Of course it is far harder for the recipient to plan what to say but even that is possible with care. Imagine that you want to hold a telephone conversation with a supplier who is known to be rather long-winded in conversation. Here are the simple steps you need to follow:

- Plan your phone conversation. Write down that plan and stick to it.
- Send a fax to the person you expect to telephone to say that you will call and to outline the headings that you wish to discuss with that person.
- Once you have entered into the conversation, put your fax in front of you. You have a very fair chance that the other person on the end of the telephone has a copy of the fax in front of him or her, too. What you have now, of course, is an agenda. Stick to your agenda.
- Take out a social contract at the beginning of the phone conversation. That simply means to agree for how long you will be talking. Of course you can't stick rigidly to it but it certainly can make a difference. If you say 'This won't take very long, only about five minutes of your time', I doubt that conversation will go on much more than five to eight minutes.
- Try during your conversation to separate chat from facts. The reason we chat on the telephone is because the telephone seems so unfriendly; it seems rather rude to plunge straight into the key subject matter we need to discuss. It is not rude to recognize that someone is busy. It is not rude to get the politenesses over quickly and then get down to the subject. Don't get involved in long conversations about the weather or general facts that you don't need to know.
- When you feel that the conversation has run for long enough and the subject matter you needed to discuss has been discussed, do your best to end the conversation. Ending conversations always seems a little impolite – as though you are hurrying away from someone because you don't want to spend time listening to that person. Now this might be the truth but the truth doesn't always rest easy upon our shoulders. A very good way to conclude a telephone conversation promptly and without giving offence is to say 'Well I realize how busy you are so I won't take any more of your time'. Nobody replies 'Oh I'm not busy, I would love to chat'; people are much more likely to say 'Right,

fine' and conclude the conversation swiftly. After all, it is hardly an insult to tell someone they are busy and therefore emphasize their own importance.

You will notice in this checklist that we have talked about making a plan. Use your **Prat** plan to plan your telephone conversation just as you planned your letter or memo.

When someone calls you, you are at a disadvantage. Perhaps what you are seeking is time to think before you speak. For this reason I am sure you chat about the weather and generalities that you don't really need to discuss in order to get your brain into gear. Don't do that. If necessary, establish that a conversation needs to be held, establish the key points that need to be covered and call back. This might look like a waste of time but in fact it is probably the most efficient way of consuming time if you are not prepared for the conversation you need to hold. There is nothing worse than listening to people talking around the subject while they are trying to get their brains into gear. Not all phone calls will need to be postponed. If at the beginning of your day you sit back and plan what you expect to happen, you will probably make a list of the phone calls you are likely to receive. Now all you need to do is to think about those phone calls in advance and think about what you would want to say to the individual who is likely to call you. Perhaps you are the recipient of frequent calls on a particular topic: having a briefing sheet on that topic and keeping it by the telephone will minimize the time wasted when one of those frequent calls comes in.

The art of communicating effectively on the telephone is to communicate with brevity and yet clarity. It boils down to short sentences, short words and simple phrases. It also boils down to listening.

HOW TO LISTEN

How interesting is the conversation you are about to listen to? If we are deeply interested in what someone else is saying we listen with all our concentration. A lot of the time in the workplace we are not especially interested, particularly if someone is talking about something which only affects us a little. This section of the chapter will show you how to listen efficiently.

In order to listen efficiently most of us need to take notes. This is particularly true when listening on the telephone. There are far too many distractions when you are talking on the telephone, particularly if someone else has entered your work area and is gesturing to you to find out how long you will be on the call. I have watched people holding telephone conversations with the phone propped up against their ear while waving someone else to come into their workspace and signing letters at the same time. It looks remarkably efficient but I don't believe for one moment they have read the letter they are signing, listened to what the person on the phone is saying or given the person entering their workspace their full attention. In fact, this is probably a triple waste of time!

To listen well, you need to make sure your brain is working properly. Your brain can work at a speed of 600 words a minute. Unfortunately, or perhaps fortunately, most people speak at a speed somewhere between 130 and 160 words a minute. If we assume an average speaking speed of 150 words a minute, you have a 450-word brain gap. And of course you have a number of options to fill that gap. Perhaps you could:

- concentrate very hard on what is being said
- think about your reply
- think about something totally different from the conversation
- fantasize
- fall asleep

From time to time we all do each of these things. That's OK, of course, if we only break concentration for 450 words in every minute. What happens is that the 450 words spread to nearer 4500 or even 45,000 – and suddenly we come to and realize that the other person has finished speaking and it is our turn to reply or in some way respond. Sadly we don't know what was being said. Taking notes not only helps you to have a record of what was said but it also allows you to extend your concentration. But taking notes longhand would be impossible: your hand probably works at a speed of about 40 words a minute and even if you have excellent shorthand you will not be making eye contact with the speaker. Part of listening is to observe wherever possible the visual messages that are being transmitted. Naturally that is not possible on the telephone but in every other listening opportunity it usually is.

So how can we take notes without missing eye contact and in a way that maximizes the use of the brain? A trick I was taught and that has worked for me all my life is to use your brain gap to analyse the words that you are hearing – to analyse them not for meaning but for parts of speech. Basically you are going to concentrate on spotting the nouns that people use. The trick is to listen for the nouns and write them down one beneath the other in a long column on the left-hand side of the page. You deliberately leave a gap on the right-hand side so that mentally you can fill in the missing words once the listening exercise is completed.

John	*will be late for the*
Meeting	*He left*
Munich	*on the 10.00*
Flight	*but the*
Plane	*took off late. He needs a*
Taxi	*to collect him from the*
Airport	

After years of using this technique I can pick up a piece of paper with a list of nouns on it and my brain will re-access the memory of what was said for up to an hour or two hours after the actual listening exercise. For most people trying it for the first time, 5, 10, maybe 20 minutes is the longest they can retain the information. But that is usually long enough, particularly if you have taken the notes as a result of a telephone conversation.

Remember, your brain has a tremendous capacity for storing information. The majority of its storage is in long-term filing. You have to design a retrieval system to get access to that filing. What your brain is not good at is holding more than seven or eight items in its short-term storage at any one time. If there are seven or eight thoughts in the short-term bit of the brain, then as soon as another thought comes along one of the earlier thoughts will be abandoned. Taking notes in this way will minimize the loss of key facts and information.

SUMMARY

If you adopt the aim of minimizing the waste of time and maximizing the value, your communication will be much more effective. Write your letters, memos and faxes with the purpose of getting them read. By all means write them long but then cut them short. Make sure that when the piece of writing lands on someone's desk it looks appetizing and readable.

When you talk on the telephone, keep that short too. Don't step away from politeness but maximize the value of the time spent on the phone. Remember that it is quite possible to use the other person's busy-ness to cut your telephone conversation short.

Remember to listen at all times. Use your brain to work on your side and not against you. Make sure that the notes you take are short and to the point and help you to recall key facts. Each of the exercises that follow will help you to achieve the key learning points from this chapter.

EXERCISES

Exercise 7.1 – Letters and faxes

You will need:

- flipchart for summarizing key points
- coloured flipchart pens
- prepared letter writing topics
- prepared letter items
- time: about one hour.

The aim of this exercise is to give the team experience in writing succinct letters. There are two ways to achieve it:

1. Take a pile of letters that you have received into the company. You might even choose to put some of your outgoing letters into this pile. Fog test them and select some of the worst: the letters that don't look readable and those that are unclear in their purpose. Select anything that has a fog score of five or over. Present these letters to the team and ask them to rewrite them using the rules from this chapter.
2. Select a list of topics for letters which the department or group normally write. Then ask individuals to prepare letters on these topics or in answer to specific incoming letters that you have received.

Obviously this part of the exercise needs to be done individually and can be done before the group meets. It should take no more than half an hour.

Once all the letters have been written, pass them around the group so that each letter moves on two places to the left. Then ask individuals to fog test the letters they have received and to look at them from the point of view of a good read and efficient use of time. While you may not have perfect letters I am sure that each letter will have some key point of value. Use the flipchart to collect the key points and to enhance the lessons learnt from the exercise.

Exercise 7.2 – Just get off this line!

You will need:

- flipchart paper
- coloured flipchart pens
- access to two telephones within the same internal network
- time: about 30–45 minutes.

The purpose of this exercise is to duplicate common phone calls received into a department or by a team. Each individual will need to role-play an incoming call. Very possibly you will ask people to role-play rambling speakers or speakers who don't get to the point. But don't forget the possibility of role-playing speakers who are very brief and to the point and from whom we find it hard to get all the information that we need. Once the role-plays have been established, set up two people on two telephone extensions. The first person will make the incoming call and will act out the part. The second person will be him or herself and will try to deal with the telephone call as efficiently as possible. If you are able to record the conversations, playing back the tape will maximize the exercise's value. If you are not able to record it, make sure the rest of the group sit either with the role-player or the recipient of the message and use them as appraisers of what is said.

The best way to run this exercise is give everyone an opportunity to receive an incoming phone call. Then on the flipchart collect all the ideas and thoughts about how those conversations could be altered. Look for common themes and common ideas as to how conversations can be politely kept to a minimum.

CHAPTER 8

MEETINGS - HOW TO MAXIMIZE THEIR VALUE

KEY LEARNING POINTS

■ Learn how to keep all discussion to the point
■ Discover how to take notes that avoid argument and ensure things happen
■ Understand the seating plan trick
■ Discover a technique for getting your agenda read

INTRODUCTION

This chapter will help you run all kinds of meetings, whether they be the formal business meeting, talking to the team, or the one-to-one 'I just want a brief word' style of meeting.

The section on organizing the agenda will help you to put the right words onto a piece of paper. There are key words that can make all the difference to the chances of an agenda being read and acted upon.

Next, the chapter will show you how to take notes that will save time and help everyone understand clearly what the meeting has agreed. The system can be used by participants or visiting note-takers alike.

The discussion on taking control in meetings will be of particular help to those who take the chair but anyone attending an uncontrolled meeting may be able to use the techniques to ensure that the participants stick to the point.

Finally, there are a number of exercises which will help you and your team members run time-efficient meetings. You can use the exercises alone or in groups, maybe even at the start of a regular team briefing.

Remember, all the tips contained in this chapter are proven to work. I have used them and taught them for over 20 years and as a result many people have saved a lot of team time and frustration.

HOW TO ORGANIZE THE AGENDA

This supposes that you intend to have an agenda. I imagine you do for the official-style meetings and probably for your team briefings too, but do you realize the value of an agenda for even a one-to-one meeting? The purpose of an agenda is simple:

- It tells the meeting participants what the meeting is about.
- It tells non-attendees what will be going on and whether they need to know what happened afterwards.
- It checklists what the meeting is for.

and when the agenda is a good one:

- It saves time.

So you need an agenda, really, for every meeting. Imagine that you pass Bill in the corridor, and the very sight of him reminds you that you must talk to him about a pressing and vital matter so you say something then and there. After all, this is good use of time, or is it? Now imagine that Bill is on his way to another meeting, or going home or even going to the loo; is he really going to listen to you with full attention? Isn't he rather thinking, just let me get rid of this person and then I can get on with whatever? Let us say he agrees to your suggestions or takes on a job from that rapid one-to-one meeting: will he remember to do it? Probably not if he is on his way home or going to another meeting which may take all memory of your encounter out of his head. And in any case, didn't you want his full attention? Maybe even the full process of thinking before he talks or agrees? There's only one way you will get that: with an agenda.

For the one-to-one meeting on a short subject the agenda is

short: it may not even be written but it's there. Try 'Bill, you and I need to talk about the Simpson contract. It shouldn't take more than ten minutes of our time, so could you come and see me in half an hour at 3.30?' Now when he turns up Bill will have looked at the relevant papers and given some thought to the matter and, what's more, he will be able to plan the rest of the day knowing how long this meeting will take. Chances are too that he will remember the meeting and what was agreed, particularly if you use the note-taking techniques listed in the next section.

So we all need agendas. Agendas to tell us what the meeting is about, agendas to help us prepare and agendas to make sure we all plan our time with an eye to the rest of the team members. An agenda is in part a social contract.

If you are not convinced that your team will see the wisdom of the agenda just ask them to list the most frustrating things about the kind of meeting I have just described. I think you'll find they list:

- waste of time
- assumption that I've got nothing else to do
- no chance to think before I'm put on the spot
- always happens at the most inconvenient moment.

Now let's turn to the agenda itself. It has to tell us what the meeting is about and to help us use time wisely. Most agendas don't do that. They simply list, often in great detail, the subject matter to be tackled and leave it at that. The perfect agenda does so much more:

1. It tells you not only the starting time of a meeting but the finishing time too. That way we can all plan our day without any false assumptions.
2. It tells you precisely what the task of the meeting is. So often this vital key point is omitted. I imagine you have seen many an agenda that talks about the pending reallocation of the car parking spaces but never uses the word *decision*.
3. It tells you how long you have to discuss, decide or trawl for ideas.
4. It gives you the key facts only and where to go for more detail if you want it.

Let's look at those four points in more detail. If I don't know the starting time of a meeting I can't get there, obviously, which is why all agendas have a starting time. But they don't specify a finishing time, not always, so how do I know when to leave? Well, I don't and the chances are I make my own plans which have nothing to do with the meeting and which might even jeopardize the meeting. Perhaps I imagine it will be all over in half an hour and make plans for something else, or even worse I plan to spend the whole day in the meeting. Either way I'll probably do my best to adjust the pace of the meeting to meet my expectations – not good for time management.

With a start time and a finish time you can now allocate time to each item. The human concentration span is about 45 minutes on average. This means that some of your meeting attendees will have switched off even at 25 minutes and others are in for the marathon. Moral of the day? Make sure that no item is to last longer than 45 minutes. And that is easy to do: all that is necessary is to break things up into digestible chunks of matter. An added bonus comes with the item meeting time; the chairman can say 'We only have 45 minutes for this so let's keep the discussion punchy'. It is as though some greater being has ordained that there is only to be 45 minutes, not the chairman herself!

There are only four possible agenda items:

- to make a *decision*
- to come up with *ideas*
- to receive *information*
- to *discuss* a subject in order to understand it better.

Let me translate them for you:

- DECISION means you'll have to make up your mind and you cannot spin it out with a load of waffle till next time.
- IDEAS means this is an ideas-gathering session *not* an ideas-knocking session; we'll evaluate ideas later. All ideas are welcome, even those that sound daft at first. (Think of Post-it™ notes and automatic doors.)
- INFORMATION means the decision has been taken and you cannot affect it, no matter how hard you try, but we are here to tell you about it and to answer questions.
- DISCUSS means just that. We are here to talk about a subject, not to make a decision. We shall have succeeded if you all understand it at the end of the meeting and are ready to take any decision necessary next time.

Try using my key words at the start of the agenda. I even put them in bold type, capitals and larger than the rest of the words so that everyone gets the message.

Figure 8.1 is an agenda that covers three of the four agenda items and it does it in one and half hours: two full concentration spans. Notice that there is a break in the middle for coffee. This is an opportunity for participants to meet and talk about anything they like

11.00 DECISION about the new offices. We have three options and must decide which of the three to select.

11.45 BREAK

11.55 IDEAS about the best way we can tackle the problem with information flow. Documents are getting stuck in the system and it is taking up to three weeks to answer customer queries.

12.20 INFORMATION about the new fault reporting system.

12.30 CLOSE

FIGURE 8.1: Agenda for a meeting of minds

and to take coffee without spilling it over each other or the papers for the meeting. Also note the order. A decision item first when everyone is fresh, followed by a well-earned break. After the break, straight in with an ideas item when people are more relaxed and more inclined to throw in any idea, however daft it sounds to them. Finally the information item, just at the point when they want to get away and so having less danger of any re-inventing of the wheel.

Figure 8.2 is a pro forma for an agenda item page.

- Key point in bullet format with minimum detail

- Key point in bullet format with minimum detail

- Key point in bullet format with minimum detail

- Key point in bullet format with minimum detail

- For more information please contact Mary Brown on extension #1234.

- Use your body language to control the meeting.

FIGURE 8.2: Agenda item #1

It makes room for only a few bullet points and it keeps the papers to an absolute minimum. A good guide would be to imagine that the people attending the meeting have not left enough time to brief themselves and are trying to read all the key information in the back of a taxi cab on the way to the meeting. In other words, use the format of an executive summary sheet that is attached to the front of a report. If you add the option of getting more information for those who are seriously under-informed or very interested in the topic, you make sure that everyone reads the agenda because it is short and those who want to know more have the opportunity to get the level of information they require.

I have used this format in many organizations, from a clearing bank to very small businesses indeed. They all find that it saves time, saves trees and, even more importantly, makes sure that the agenda papers are actually read!

Now stop and think what is missing from my agenda:

- *Any other business*   This cannot be a good item; if it is raised without preparation how can anyone take a reasonable decision or make realistic valuable comment?
- *Matters arising from the minutes of the last meeting*   Simply an opportunity to reopen long-completed discussion.

Exercise 8.1 later in this chapter gives you an opportunity to get your team to write the perfect agenda for your purposes.

THE TRICK OF NOTE-TAKING

In most of the meetings I have attended, some poor soul is given the job of trying to take notes that will be acceptable to the other members of the meeting. Indeed, often the first item on the agenda is matters arising from the last meeting (something that you will note is definitely missing from my agenda) and this takes up half the time of the meeting, during which participants argue about what it was they agreed last time. We can solve that terrible waste of time. It only happens because the minutes of the meeting come as a surprise to the participants at the meeting. Now the reason they come as a surprise is that they don't match with the secret version written by each of the participants. And the reason they don't match is that everyone nods off from time to time in a meeting or gets bored with a subject that holds little interest for them and lets their minds wander.

By all means give the job of taking the minutes to a member of the meeting but give them a flipchart too, and ask them to take the minutes of the meeting on the flipchart for all to see. This has three major effects:

- The minutes are kept short as no one wants to write for hours on a flipchart.
- The minutes are agreed as we go because everyone looks at the flipchart as it is being written up or at least at some stage during the meeting. If they think it is an unfair record they tend to say so then and there.

- The minutes are written by all the participants of the meeting as people tend to say 'Get this down on the chart' or 'I think we ought to add this to the minutes', which means that the note-taker's job is easier.

It works. It works even better if you use one of those whiteboards which also acts as a photocopier; you can take sufficient copies for each person to be given a set of minutes as they leave. Of course this is not essential, just a frill. With good handwritten minutes on the flipchart you can either shrink them on the photocopier or in no time at all they can be typed into the computer.

Sometimes the individual chosen to take the minutes objects to taking them so visibly. Tell them not to worry: with this system the whole meeting helps the note-taker. The secretary of an accountant in one of the five clearing banks takes minutes for her boss's meeting this way. At first she was worried but now she is relieved because it saves her so much time. Before using this system she used to take the best notes she could of a meeting which was all about something she did not understand. Then she would type them out and go and check her version with a member of the meeting. All this took a lot of time and meant that the minutes were often very late in being published. Now all she has to do is to pause when she does not understand something and one of the meeting participants tells her what to write!

A good tip is to prepare flipchart paper before the meeting with headers showing the topic to be minuted. If you take along plenty of Blu-tak™ the completed minutes can be stuck to the wall as you go. That way everyone keeps the full picture in their mind.

HOW TO TAKE CONTROL IN MEETINGS

First let us assume you are chairing the meeting. This is, after all, a position of control. There are a number of simple things you can do to make sure the meeting uses time efficiently:

- Publish your agenda three working days before the meeting. If you use the format shown above, it will be read.
- Organize a seating plan that takes account of the way people behave in meetings.
- Make sure that the meeting has a set of rules and that everyone follows the rules.
- Use the agenda to control participants' involvement and interest.
- Use the timing to control the garrulous and encourage the silent.
- Use your body language to control the meeting.

Take the seating plan first of all. King Arthur was right: a round table is the best way to hold a meeting. That way we are all equal participants and everyone can see everyone else. It makes it difficult to nod off or to hold side conversations. If you also plan who sits where, you can control the meeting very subtly.

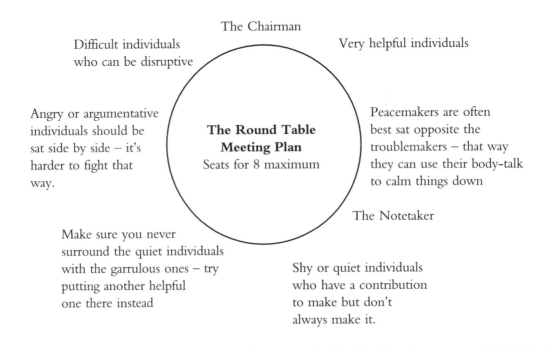

The Chairman

Difficult individuals who can be disruptive

Very helpful individuals

Angry or argumentative individuals should be sat side by side – it's harder to fight that way.

The Round Table Meeting Plan
Seats for 8 maximum

Peacemakers are often best sat opposite the troublemakers – that way they can use their body-talk to calm things down

The Notetaker

Make sure you never surround the quiet individuals with the garrulous ones – try putting another helpful one there instead

Shy or quiet individuals who have a contribution to make but don't always make it.

FIGURE 8.3: A round table meeting plan

Notice in Figure 8.3 how the individuals have been placed according to their known temperament. This may not be very subtle after a while but it certainly helps the meeting. If you regularly hold team meetings, why not discuss the contribution you each make to the meeting and accept the sobriquets you attach one to another? Sometimes I use a team roles questionnaire with groups so that they can see how each can help the other by using their team strengths. The common roles played by team members are:

- *Leader* who organizes the group.
- *Motivator* who keeps spirits up and tasks moving along.
- *Creator* who comes up with original ideas.
- *Innovator* who adapts other people's ideas.
- *Manager* who manages the people.

- *Organizer* who manages the tasks.
- *Evaluator* who spots the flaws in the ideas.
- *Finisher* who makes sure that things actually get done.

Within the exercises later in the chapter there is an opportunity for team members to consider the roles they play and how to use them to maximize value in a meeting.

Rules in meetings should be written by the participants to the meeting. If yours is a regular team-briefing session then members of the team will need to make sure that they design a set of rules to help each other maximize the contribution made. No outsider can set the rules of a meeting but a good set of rules would certainly contain the following:

- Never, even if you are a known evaluator, put down a colleague's ideas in a negative fashion. Ask a question instead; it has the same effect, causing the individual to think again, but this time it feels constructive.
- Always turn up on time to a meeting and give the meeting your full attention while you are there.
- Allow everyone to make a contribution. This is often best done by going around the group to hear an opinion from each person present at the start of a topic and once again just as you are about to take the decision.
- Keep an open mind to the contributions of others, even if you think you have a really good idea. The best way to do this is to write down your ideas on a sheet of paper so that your brain can concentrate on what it hears, not on what it is trying to hold on to.
- Don't get sidetracked by something that is not relevant to the meeting or contains so much detail that it should be dealt with by a separate working party outside the meeting.
- Admit ownership of the problem being discussed by the meeting. Don't leave it to the rest of the participants if it does not affect you or your department.
- Use a flipchart to draw up a decision-making chart (Figure 8.4) to ensure that all the decisions are acceptable to all members of the meeting and will be enacted.

Possible solutions suggested	Effect of the best possible outcome	Effect of the worst possible outcome	Likelihood of best possible outcome Scale 1–10 10 is high
We provide a smoking room	Smokers smoke in the smoking room. Everyone is happy	Time is wasted by smokers and non-smokers are dissatisfied because they get no breaks	6
The firm provides hypnosis for all smokers to help them give up	All smokers give up within six months	It costs a lot of money and it does not work	4
We sack all smokers because they are a health hazard to others	A no-smoking office	Industrial tribunals for unfair dismissal. All smokers reinstated	1
We leave things as they are	Smokers are happy	Non-smokers sue the company for passive smoking damage to health	7
We allow people to smoke in their own offices	Provided the office door is shut and they do not smoke when non-smokers visit – happiness	The air conditioning might transfer the smoke around the building	7
We provide humidifiers for all smokers and discourage smoking	Only the totally addicted will continue smoking. The effect of smoke minimized	Cost of humidifiers. The office still smells of smoke at times	8
We offer new jobs to non-smokers and ban smoking in the office	No smoking	Smokers leave or spend time in the street smoking and looking untidy	7

FIGURE 8.4: Decision chart for a decision about smoking in the office

Not all topics on a business agenda are going to interest all of the participants equally. Some topics are very boring to many of the participants. So organize the agenda to make sure that the variety of topics is kept fresh and that those who only need to attend for part of the meeting can do so without problems.

If the agenda has been set with time limits for each topic it is possible to use those time limits to control the meeting, particularly the garrulous members of the meeting. Allocate a maximum time for a speaker to speak at any one time. Usually two minutes is quite long enough for anyone to say what they have to say, especially if they realize that they will have plenty of other chances to add more later. Then ask a garrulous member to take control of the time each speaker speaks, by holding up a pen to signify the end of two minutes. And when that person comes to speak just watch how the whole meeting controls the time he or she takes!

But what if you are not the chairman of a meeting and yet you want to control the way the meeting goes? Can you use any of these ideas?

Of course you might be able to influence the seating plan simply by turning up early to the meeting and encouraging people to sit where you feel they would be able to make the best contribution. Perhaps you could suggest the need for meeting rules and then make sure that they include some of the ideas I have listed. If you are the note-taker you could probably influence the meeting by insisting on working with a flipchart because you find it easier. Then you could draw up the decision chart as a matter of course. Perhaps you could even suggest the two-minute rule so that everyone may have a turn in the discussion; then you could take control of the pen and the timing.

Probably the best control comes from your own willingness to give your best to the meeting and your concern for the best use of team time.

SUMMARY

Meetings are the most efficient way of communicating to a group of people all at once. They ensure a team stays together, they reinforce group decisions and they provide a valuable forum, but they can be the biggest and most expensive waste of time of all. By controlling the agenda and taking the minutes of the meeting in an open fashion you will limit the time wasting. What is more, you'll all enjoy the meetings so much more. This chapter has shown you how to give your best in a meeting and how to maximize the value of the time given by the participants. To get the most from this chapter you now need to work through some, if not all, of the exercises that follow.

EXERCISES

Exercise 8.1 – Write an agenda

The purpose of this exercise is to help team members appreciate the value of an agenda for all types of meetings. Use it as the first exercise and maybe use it at the start of a team-briefing meeting before you talk about this chapter.

You will need:

- flipcharts
- coloured flipchart pens.

Place at least one flipchart (preferably one per three people involved) somewhere accessible to all participants.

Make a list of topics that are important to your team at the moment. Perhaps you are an organization that is thinking of banning smoking; maybe you are trying to change a system or introduce a new company philosophy. Try to make sure the items you list matter to the individuals involved in the exercise. Make sure they are not just decision items but add in other types too. Now ask team members to list anything they think is important and should be dealt with by the team, anything they are worried about or want to change.

Ask the team to draw up a list of the items on one of the flipcharts. Take the most complicated subject about which a decision should be made and set the team to discuss it. Let the discussion roam free without your interruption or ideas. After 20 minutes ask them what they have achieved. Ask people to talk about their hidden agendas and whether they think the discussion was good or a waste of time.

Next, ask them what they want to achieve if they discuss another topic. Let them pick the topic and the required end result. Draft up the topic onto an agenda sheet on another flipchart in the style suggested in the text of this chapter. Now set the meeting going again but this time take note of how the meeting works and whether it sticks to the point. See who brings the meeting back to order (someone will) and how long it takes them to achieve their desired result.

Exercise 8.2 – Setting an agenda from a list of topics

Use this exercise immediately after Exercise 8.1 and after you have discussed agendas, as covered earlier in this chapter. A suggested answer is given on page 140. You will need:

- flipcharts
- coloured flipchart pens.

Now invite the team, in groups of no more than three, to create an agenda that will achieve all the following things within a 90-minute meeting. Assume this is a list of items to be dealt with by the General Administration department:

- A new car park is opening up for staff. We need to make sure the spaces (48) are allocated fairly among the departments (Accounts 12, Sales 20, Maintenance 3, Production 42, Managing Directors' Office 9, Reception & Switchboard 4, Secretaries 10). The existing car park has 112 spaces only, allocated to 8 directors and 2 sales staff.
- Accounts have designed a new budget pack that will affect everyone at the meeting: they want to explain it to all.
- The number of customer complaints has been rising recently. Most of the complaints are about the new documentation sent out with sales. It has changed significantly and been designed by an outside consultant. You are the department responsible for this form and can change it if you wish.
- A new contract is to be awarded for the company canteen which is opening in one month's time. Five companies have tendered for the contract.
- Your boss has asked for the team's views on cancelling the office Christmas party this year and either donating a sum of money to charity in lieu of the function or running a summer event.

Exercise 8.3 – What did we just agree?

The purpose of this exercise is to demonstrate how taking minutes on a flipchart can improve the minutes of a meeting.
You will need:

- one flipchart
- coloured flipchart pens

- pencils and paper for each team member.

Ask each member of the team to make notes from the following information. Read out the information once only and at a normal speaking pace. Make it like a meeting that is taking place. There are four people involved in the meeting you will be reading about. If you can involve three others in reading out the material, each taking a character, so much the better but it is not essential.

The Meeting

Margaret from Accounts, Peter from Administration, Ratan from IT and Larry from Marketing are holding a meeting. The main purpose of the meeting is to make a decision about standardizing the computer systems used by the various departments. Marketing, Accounts and Administration have different systems; IT have been asked to standardize the whole network within the next six months. Now read the following to your team members. Do not treat the bold text differently.

This meeting is between Margaret from Accounts, Peter from Administration and Larry from Marketing. They have invited Ratan from It to attend. Each of the three departments has a different computer system, this is seen as time consuming and unnecessary. Ratan will help them change over to a unified system, but which system will it be?

Ratan	Why don't you start by telling me about the **advantages of your present systems** as you see them?
Larry	Our system is used as a **multi-faceted database and it keeps account of over 8000 names on-line at any one time. It enables us to select customers by up to 48 different fields and customize the marketing material we send to them.** It works well because it is fast and efficient and quite frankly I see no point in fixing something that isn't broken.
Margaret	Accounts has a good system. It is a little slow and we **have been using it for five years** now. Everyone understands it and we have got rid of all the bugs. I am very reluctant to change anything at all because the last time we changed we had six months of hell

trying to get the figures right and we very nearly had a qualified audit report because the audit trail was not complete. It uses **a 480 machine and** I'm sure everyone can access it provided we give them the right **passwords**.

Peter We use the **state-of-the-art Macintosh full laser colour Quark software to desktop publish** all the material we need for the **various users in the organization**. No way are we going back to PCs and Windows, thank you.

Ratan OK, so you all want to stick to your existing systems but they are not compatible. Margaret, you need **everyone to sign off purchase orders before processing invoices for payment but they have to be done manually at present**. With a new standardized system we could process them on-line.

Margaret The **last thing I want is every Tom, Dick and Harry going on-line into the accounts package** to interfere with our figures. No thank you we'll stick to what we've got.

Peter I don't see why we need to spoil our perfect desktop publishing for accounts invoices; can't they sort it out themselves? What does it matter anyway?

Margaret Oh come on, Peter, if you don't approve purchase notes we don't pay suppliers and you don't get any more supplies. Anyway the **figures are essential for the month-end accounts and for sending to Head Office**.

Larry What I need is an **on-line database with access to 12,000 names**. Maybe 60 fields to sort. **I'll change to anything that gives me that**. We don't care what the system is as long as it works for us. After all, no customers and you don't need to worry about the accounts being accurate – there won't be any company to write accounts for.

Ratan 12,000 names on-line the whole time . . . that's a lot, do you really need all that? And why 60 fields?

Larry	OK, say **5000 names on-line and access to the others with minimum hassle**, but I need those fields.
Ratan	60?
Larry	Well we use 36 at the moment and we're bound to think up other uses as time goes by.
Ratan	You really **use 36 fields to sort on**?
Larry	**We use 20 all the time, the others are used once or twice a year**. But I'm not giving up what we've got, the others would have my guts for garters. Anyway it's a good system.
Margaret	Surely you are not suggesting that we change to the system used by Marketing? That would be out-rageous – after all, it's only a glorified database.
Larry	And your old-fashioned accounts system isn't?
Margaret	My old-fashioned accounts system, as you call it, is a proper **system written for us by JH Consultants to make sure that we comply with all current legislation**.
Ratan	And does it? Comply with all the newer legislation that is? Haven't there been some changes recently?
Margaret	Well, we had to tweak the figures a bit last year and the **auditors have given me a long list of requirements, most of which will have to be manual journal adjustments** but no, I am still happy with the system. Besides my **team work flat out: they haven't got time for parallel running and learning a new system**. And the changes you talk about simply mean more work for the accounts department.
Ratan	So a **new system might be timely if it were able to adapt to all the legislation changes**?
Margaret	Oh yes and I'm willing to commission JH Con-sultants to start writing add-ons now.
Peter	Excuse me, has everyone forgotten the needs of the administration department? We have to produce

perfect material and without our brand-new top-of-the-range kit we can't do it. I've **just spent thousands on a new colour laser printer**; it is state of the art, can't change it now.

Ratan Maybe you don't have to change – have you got Powermacs? **Are you IBM compatible**?

Peter **We've got one Powermac.**

Ratan **Would you find access to Larry's database useful?**

Peter We might, a darn sight more useful than access to an accounts package!

Margaret Look Peter, if you don't match up to the needs of the accounts department there won't be any need for fancy newsletters and pretty presentation programs, I can tell you.

Larry Hell, look at the time, I've got to go. Do what you like as long as you leave my database alone or better still expand it for me.

Margaret I think we should do nothing. Leave things as they are. After all it works well at present.

Peter I agree with that. We're quite happy. If I really need to do budgets then I can fill them in on bits of paper and give them to the experts.

Ratan But the **whole aim of this meeting was to make recommendations for change. The board wants to see a new compatible networked system and I've got the budget for it.**

Larry
Margaret } Was it? Nobody said so.
Peter

Once you have read this out to your team ask them to tell you the key points from the meeting and what decision could be taken about the new computer system. Don't be surprised if different people have different ideas about what was said.

Next, go through the story again and this time stop and ask

someone to make a note on the flipchart every time you read out the statements typed in bold.

Now discuss with your team how that meeting could have been better organized and how the decision should be taken.

Exercise 8.4 – Team roles

The role a person plays has nothing to do with the task he or she undertakes. The role is more a reflection on the way that person tackles the task, perhaps indicative of character or attitude to a task. In a team, different roles are necessary to help the team members take the decisions they need to take and make things work best.

This exercise is about helping your team members understand their natural roles. It could be done scientifically with the help of a team roles questionnaire (available from Management Learning Resources Limited, PO Box 28, Carmarthen, Dyfed SA31 1DT, UK) but you may prefer to let people think about their preferred roles in a more relaxed manner.

You will need:

- a flipchart
- coloured flipchart pens
- a prepared flipchart showing the following team roles:
  - *Leader* who organizes the group
  - *Motivator* who keeps spirits up and tasks moving along
  - *Creator* who comes up with original ideas
  - *Innovator* who adapts other people's ideas
  - *Manager* who manages the people
  - *Organizer* who manages the tasks
  - *Evaluator* who spots the flaws in the ideas
  - *Finisher* who makes sure that things actually get done
- paper and pencils for each participant.

Ask the team members to look at the list of roles and write down all their names at the bottom of their sheets of paper and the roles (one per person) they think best describes them at the top.

Next, just like the game of consequences, tell them to fold over the top of their sheets of paper and pass them along in a clockwise direction, making sure that the name of the individual shows at all times.

The next person should write down the role that best describes the person named on the bottom of the sheet of paper just received. Once everyone has done that, they should fold over the paper to hide what they have written and pass the sheets on to the participant on their left.

When the sheets are completed, all the team members will have a piece of paper with their view of their own team role and the views others have of their team role. Since no role is bad and no role is better than another the discussion that follows is looking only for strengths.

Once a team role has been decided upon for everyone, encourage each participant to make up a label from a folded piece of card with his or her name on it and the preferred role (Figure 8.5). This card should be taken into meetings to make sure that the meeting always listens to participants when they are using their strengths.

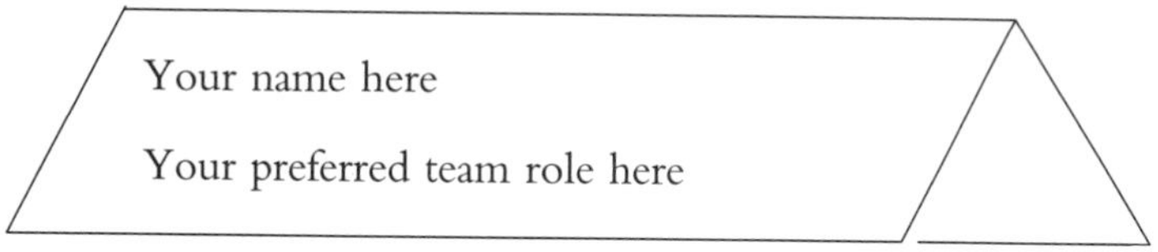

Your name here

Your preferred team role here

FIGURE 8.5: Name card

Exercise 8.5 – Team rules

The purpose of this exercise is to help the team set a list of rules that will help them run efficient meetings.

You will need:

- flipcharts
- coloured flipchart pens
- a pre-prepared list of the possible rules the team could adopt.

Possible rules for the meeting could include:

- Never, even if you are a known evaluator, put down a colleague's ideas in a negative fashion. Ask a question instead.
- Always turn up on time to a meeting and give the meeting your full attention while you are there.
- Allow everyone to make a contribution.
- Keep an open mind to the contributions of others even if you think you have a really good idea.
- Don't get sidetracked by something that is not relevant to the meeting or is in so much detail that it should be dealt with by a separate working party outside the meeting.

- Admit ownership of the problem being discussed by the meeting.
- Use a flipchart to draw up a decision-making chart to ensure that all the decisions are acceptable to all members of the meeting and will be enacted.

Place at least one flipchart (preferably one per three people involved) somewhere accessible to all.

Ask the team to use one flipchart to note down the things that annoy them most in meetings and another chart to note down the things they like best about your meetings.

Next, using the list above as a base, help the team set a list of meeting rules. Once the list is complete and collected on a third flipchart, make sure you have everyone's agreement. Take the list and have it typed up and then give a laminated copy to each team member. Take one copy along to all meetings and display it prominently.

SUGGESTED ANSWER TO EXERCISE 8.2

General Administration Department Meeting

AGENDA

Time in minutes	Topic
35	DECISION as to which of the five contenders should be awarded the catering contract.
10	BREAK
25	DISCUSSION – What is wrong with the new sales documentation? DECISION – How shall we proceed?
10	IDEAS for a Christmas Party replacement.
10	INFORMATION about the new budget pack. (Accounts Dept.)

CHAPTER 9

DROP-IN VISITORS AND DELEGATION

KEY LEARNING POINTS

- Learn how to avoid interruptions
- Discover the part that office layout plays
- Learn the art of clear delegation
- Learn how to avoid upward delegation

INTRODUCTION

This chapter will help you avoid interruptions of any sort. Since part of the reason for those interruptions is often delegation gone wrong, it will also look at the art of delegation. Not everyone has someone to whom they can delegate but more people do have the opportunity of delegation than they think. Perhaps you can pass a task outside the department or even outside the organization – that is only another form of delegation, after all.

The section on office layouts will show you some nightmare examples of office layout that prevent good time management and how to work with them even if you can't alter them. It will also show you the style of layout you should be aiming for if you want to preserve good time management.

The section on handling interruptions politely and firmly shows you how to deal with drop-in visitors so that they do not feel offended and yet go away until you want them.

The discussion on delegating effectively will help you to explain tasks in such a way that anyone can understand what you want to be done and what success will look like.

Finally, there are a number of exercises that will help you and your team members keep interruptions to a minimum. You can use the exercises alone or in groups, maybe even at the start of a regular team briefing.

These tips work. And what is more, they do not offend people; some of them even make it fun to manage time.

THE OFFICE LAYOUT – ITS PART IN YOUR DOWNFALL

When I first went to work most people seemed to have the luxury of an office to themselves. It meant that we all got on with what we were doing and took a break when the tea lady came round with tea and buns. It was lonely but it seemed to work. If you wanted a chat you went to see someone in his or her office and if you didn't want anyone to drop in on you then you shut your door and there you could stay all day uninterrupted.

But those little boxes did not make for teamwork. We all did our own thing, never consulting one another. Nor did those little boxes make for good use of office space. Office space was not at a premium then, so it did not matter. Soon it will not be at a premium again, as more and more organizations slim down the staff and more and more people work from home and become teleworkers. So maybe it won't matter in the future either.

But, for now, the problem of office space is threefold:

- *Open plan offices* make for good teamwork but by definition are noisy and full of interruptions.
- *Shared offices*, often with two or three people crammed into a tiny space, make it difficult to work without interruptions.
- The luxury of the *solo office* has problems of isolation for those who like to feel part of the team.

Anyone who works from home probably falls into the third category simply because there is no one else there to work with, although the family can be frequent drop-in visitors. I know, I work from home part of the time.

Take the open plan office first. It saves money, it saves space and it builds teams but it is noisy and often hard to work in. Office

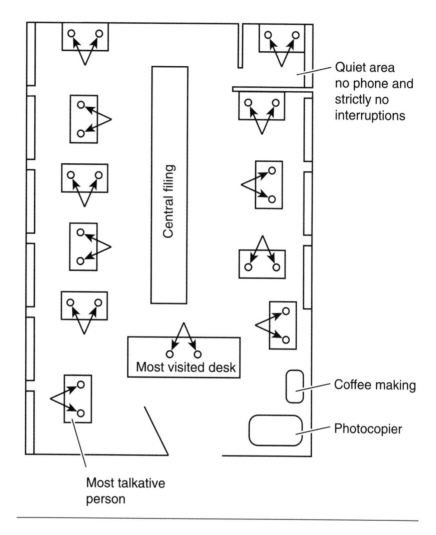

FIGURE 9.1: The open plan office

designers have maximized the use of space but not the use of time. The plugs cannot be moved, the computers must be in a certain space; because of this I am aware that what I consider to be the perfect layout (Figure 9.1) may well not be possible for you to achieve. Have a look at the ideas anyway and see if any of them can be adapted for your open plan office. Exercise 9.1 gives the team a chance to design an efficient office starting from where they are now.

Of course no two offices are alike but in Figure 9.1 I have imagined windows down the two long sides and a door at one end. Most of the symbols I have used are obvious but the double-arrow with two circles symbol shows the direction of the eyeballs of the person sitting at the desk. The key interrupters are:

- the telephone
- other people's conversations
- people chatting at the photocopier
- the act of filing
- automatic eyeball contact

and the most important point in avoiding interruptions is avoiding automatic eye contact. We are polite people generally and if someone looks at us we become aware of their eyes and feel the need to look back. Think of holidays in countries where they try to sell you trinkets. All the trinket seller wants is to make eye contact with you, then he knows he can sell you something. If you are even more polite and say 'No thank you' he knows in what language to approach you. If he fails to make eye contact within about 30 seconds he moves on to the next person. He doesn't feel insulted – just prefers not to waste his time on you. Similarly, your colleagues will not feel insulted if you do not automatically make eye contact, they will merely assume you are busy and either get on with their work or go and talk to someone else.

Look at all the desks in Figure 9.1: they are arranged so that no eyeball automatically disturbs another, unlike the horror situation portrayed in Figure 9.2 that I see so often. With this layout it is very difficult to avoid eye contact. One person looks up and mutters something and all the others feel that they too should look up and acknowledge the interrupter. One phone rings and they all hear the conversation.

Now look at Figure 9.1 again and you can see that all the eyes are looking away not just from other eyeballs but from the natural interruption areas too. Except, that is, the eyes of the person sitting at the most visited desk. Perhaps this person deals with expenses or

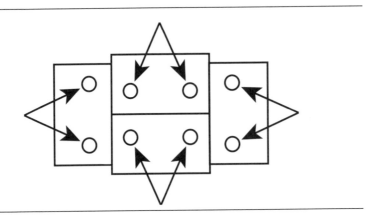

FIGURE 9.2: The worst possible desk set-up

general queries, or acts as receptionist to the team; the desk is facing the entrance and indeed forms a barrier against entry to the rest of the room. Close by this individual are the natural interrupters: photocopier, kettle and any other items that mean people have to stand and wait for machinery to work. Of course, while we stand and wait we chat. To the left of the doorway is the desk of the noisiest person in the team. Sitting that person there may not always be possible but if it can be done it does keep the major noise in one area. Of course it is not especially conducive for that individual to work but that may be a small price to pay. The desk could always be reversed to make the eyeballs look out of the window and not into the room.

At the back of the room to the right, you have a quiet area: no phones, no files, no noise, just a desk and a chair that can be booked by anyone in the open plan office for getting on with a special piece of work. This is not to be used as a meeting room or for a private chat. The only time you interrupt here is if there has been a fire alarm or something similar. Finally, the central filing causes a barrier between the two halves of the room, keeping noise down and yet accessible to all. Central filing in itself is a time-saver, as those who have worked through Chapter 6 will know.

Telephones are a major nuisance in an open plan office. At the least, turn down the ringing so that they ring loud enough for the relevant person to hear but not so loud that the office sounds like an old-fashioned switchboard. Even better, get phones with flashing lights instead of bells. They can be seen but they interrupt only the person for whom the call is intended. None of these telephone tricks will prevent you from carrying out the client care requirement of answering in three rings but each will minimize the interruption caused by a ringing phone. Indeed, even if your organization does not have the rule of answering within three rings, it is a good thing to introduce since it cuts the interruption level. Make sure everyone answers in three rings or, if you are making an internal call, hang up after hearing four rings through the handset.

Of course if you have the luxury of an office to yourself you can maximize the time aspects with your layout. But, please, not like the one shown in Figure 9.3. The occupant of the totally misused office will be interrupted by anyone who wanders past because most people who see an open door look in out of curiosity. Once the eyeballs have looked in, the interruption is made. Even if a mini-meeting is going on and the door is open or glassed, a drop-in visitor can assume it is ok to pop in and put things on your desk. How much more sensible to lay the office out like the one shown in Figure 9.4. Now the casual passer by looks in and sees the back of the head of someone

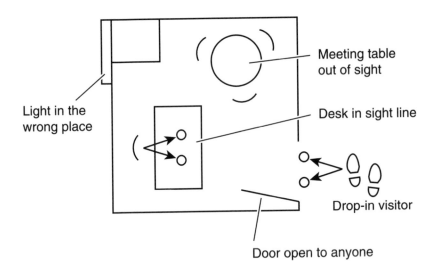

Meeting table
out of sight

Light in the
wrong place

Desk in sight line

Drop-in visitor

Door open to anyone

FIGURE 9.3: The luxury of an office to yourself – totally misused

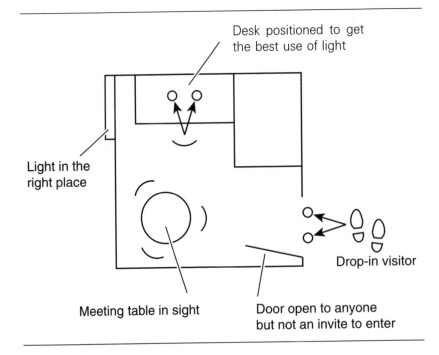

Desk positioned to get
the best use of light

Light in the
right place

Drop-in visitor

Meeting table in sight

Door open to anyone
but not an invite to enter

FIGURE 9.4: The luxury of an office to yourself – well used

working and thinks 'I'll come back later when he/she is not so busy'. If a meeting is in progress, even with glass in the door it is obvious.

Since many open plan or shared offices cannot be organized in this way and even some solo offices do not lend themselves to good time-orientated use of space, the next section contains a few tips to help – whatever the office looks like.

HOW TO HANDLE INTERRUPTIONS POLITELY BUT FIRMLY

Why not shut the door? If you work in an office on your own it is so simple. But I know that people do not shut the door. Sometimes the office is so small it seems claustrophobic, sometimes too hot, sometimes it just feels lonely. Many people who have offices to themselves would rather sit in the big open plan office and vice versa. The managing director of a client of mine chooses to sit in the open office with part of his team; it keeps him near to the action and it makes him approachable.

But do remember that for most of us interruptions are part of our job. We have to deal with them and must make time for them. If you plan your day to the full with no time left for interruptions, then any single interruption is a nuisance. If you plan your day with a slot for interruptions and no interruptions happen then you can get ahead of your schedule with extra work, spend the time thinking or even reading another chapter of this book.

Keep all interruptions short. Ask 'how long will this take?' and time it. Say 'I can give this five minutes and no more'. Keep interruptions short by sticking to the point and avoiding general social chatter as a prelude to something more important. And if you need to interrupt someone, make a list of the key points you need to discuss and take it with you so that the other person can see how organized you are. In fact if you go to someone else's office or space it is easier to walk away when you have finished, so try to interrupt rather than be interrupted – if you can control your own chatter level, that is. Remember you are entering into a social contract when you interrupt. Keep that contract short and to the point and stick to any contract you make. Others may not value your interruption as highly as you do.

So what do you do when interruptions come? The first part of the solution is to find out why you receive interruptions: are they vital, inevitable or due to some other cause? Are they from the same people, regular or random? To find out, keep a log of interruptions for at least a week. Your log must make a note of:

- who interrupts
- at what time of day they interrupt
- why they interrupt

After a week you may find a pattern emerging:

- Perhaps people interrupt you at a certain time, maybe at a time when you are feeling restless and more inclined to look up at the eyeballs as they pass. Maybe you need to take a break from work at a particular time of the day. If so, organize interruptions for that time; you'll be grateful for them and will settle back to work more easily afterwards.
- Perhaps the interruptions are all coming from the same people or from different people about the same matter. If this is so maybe you need to arrange a regular meeting to discuss general points, either one to one or with the group.
- Maybe the interruptions are telling you that you ask people to check with you too often, or that you have delegated badly or possibly not delegated enough.
- Perhaps certain members of your team are unsure of their tasks or maybe unsure of themselves.

The solutions will all be different but now that you know the reasons for the interruptions you can do something about them.

If the interruptions are all from within the organization, and particularly if they are from within your team, decide the best time of day to be interrupted and tell everyone that is when you'll be available to them. If people know when you are available they tend to wait for the next slot in the timetable rather than interrupt unless something is truly urgent. Of course this assumes that you have dealt with the lessons of Chapter 4 on prioritizing.

Many years ago I sat in a large office working on a tricky task throughout August. Now August was a quiet month for my colleagues so they tended to drop by every so often for a chat. Sometimes a very useful chat, one that would lead to new opportunities, but nevertheless an interruption that meant that I had to work all the harder to catch up with my task. One day in desperation, because my deadline was approaching all too fast, I put up a sign on my door that said:

> Behind this door is someone
> working on a complicated task
> PLEASE come in and
> HELP

I saw no one all day. All I heard was approaching footsteps, a low murmur as they read the notice and then the sound of hastily retreating footsteps. In fact I got so lonely that I stuck my head out of the office at five o'clock only to be told, '... thought you were busy'. Nor do you actually need an office door on which to pin the notice. A lawyer client of mine who works in an open plan office has a notice on a stand by her desk that says:

> The Lawyer is
> BUSY
> Please come again later

When she turns the notice around, it says:

> The Lawyer is
> IN
> and available for consultation.

The gentle humour gives the message and stops any wounded feelings.

An open plan office is more difficult when it comes to interruptions but even then there are ways to let people know you are busy and not ignoring them out of bad feelings for them. First we all need to know each other's busy periods. Next we have to choose a symbol that says: 'I'm busy right now, call later. Some teams I know put up small flags on miniature desktop poles, others put messages on their screen-savers, but the most visible and possibly most effective of all is the red cap approach. When I wear my red cap it means 'I'm busy. Please let me get on with this task in hand'. Not as daft as it sounds: this idea is very visible, a bit of fun and it works.

If someone comes into your office or space to interrupt, stand up and remain standing; whatever you do don't offer them a hot drink – it will take a long time to serve, cool and consume. By the way, it is not rude to stand up, actually it looks very welcoming but if you are worried pass it off by getting up to fetch something or close a door or window and then remain standing. If you go to someone else's office refuse the offer of a seat by saying 'I've been sitting down all day, need to stretch my back a bit, if you don't mind'. Incidentally, standing even to answer the phone helps you keep your conversation short and makes you stick to the point. Make it one of the good habits you develop.

When the interruption is over, get right back to work. This is habit too and many of us turn a short interruption into a long one by muttering to anyone who will listen about the interruption we just experienced or even by using it as an excuse to get up and do something else. Chapter 5 on procrastination will help you here.

HOW TO DELEGATE EFFECTIVELY

Not all of us have someone to whom we can delegate but those who do often fail either to delegate well or even to delegate at all. If your log of interruptions recorded a large number of queries about a task you had delegated then you are a poor delegator in the eyes of your delegatees and those are the eyes that count. Sometimes lack of entries in the interruptions log means that you have not delegated enough. Maybe under the time teamwork session you will find that you are doing a lot of tasks that others could do better. Try the quiz in Exercise 9.3 to see if you are delegating enough.

Delegation involves a lot of things:

- *Risk* that the task will not be done as well as it used to be at least for a short period of time during the learning curve.
- *Giving up hobby tasks* that you enjoy but you know someone else could do as well as you do, if not better.
- *Handing on part of your job* to someone who one day might take all of your job.
- *Risk* the delegatee will do that task better than you ever did.
- *Losing the feeling of being in control* because everything no longer passes through your hands.
- *Patience* because it always takes at least five times as long to delegate a task for the first time as it would to do it yourself.

Which means the delegator and the delegatee have both to be ready for the experience. There are two key ingredients to delegation:

- authority
- power

If either is missing then something will go wrong with the delegation. First, the authority: anyone who undertakes a task has the authority to do that task. That authority may be enshrined in their job specification or it may have been usurped at some time in the past but is theirs by right now. Giving the task to someone else without giving them the authority only means that the task will keep coming back to the delegator because outsiders will not allow the full delegation to take place. Just try asking someone to take messages for you without telling those who leave messages that it is all right to speak to your message-taker. No one leaves a message, the message-taker gets frustrated and you lose out. If you want others to accept the authority you have given to your delegatee you must tell them about the new authority vested in the individual concerned. Sometimes you will even have to negotiate for that authority itself.

For example, you may want someone to be able to claim expenses or to be the recipient of information from others.

Authority does not mean complete abdication at once; it is available at eight levels (Figure 9.5). You have to decide at which level you are delegating the authority. Perhaps in the early stages of the task the level of authority is only at level 1, rising quickly to level 4 and then taking time to reach level 6. But remember that in order to make it easier for the act of delegation to succeed you must delegate enough authority for the task to be accomplished successfully. And once you have delegated the task with anything higher than level 3 authority do not undercut, overrule or in any way arbitrarily reverse the other person's decision, even if you don't like it or would not have taken it that way. If you are worried that you will not be able to control a task once delegated, perhaps you should not delegate it after all or perhaps you should limit the level of authority.

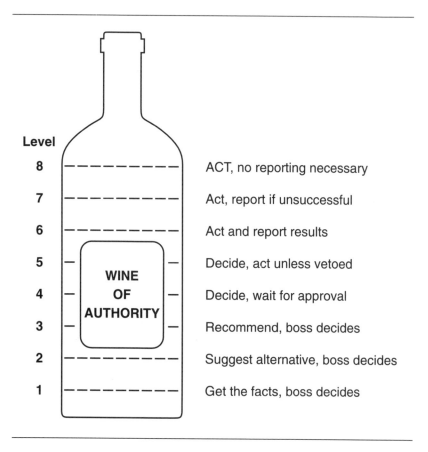

FIGURE 9.5: Eight levels of authority

The next essential ingredient of delegation is power. Power is simply the ability – mental, technical and physical – to undertake the task. If I do not have a driving licence I should not have the task delegated to me of moving customers' cars; something is bound to go wrong. Most power is handed on at delegation but certain tasks assume a level of basic understanding and it pays to check that the necessary level of understanding is present. In other words, don't ask the house painter to restore the Sistine chapel unless he also happens to have a degree in art restoration.

A word of warning: although you can and must set up a line of responsibility from the delegatee to you, you cannot abdicate your own responsibility for a job just because you delegated it. That is why Chief Executive Officers are sacked when one of their subordinates makes a mistake. It is also why the Managing Director is responsible for replenishing the supply of loo rolls in the toilets (but I don't recommend asking him to carry out the task personally).

HOW TO DELEGATE

DEFINE THE TASK

Write down how you do the task, then put your checklist away for 24 hours, take it out and follow your own instructions. Now make the necessary corrections. This is the simplest way to make absolutely sure that you have all the necessary detail written down. It is no use writing 'switch on the computer' if your computer has a particular figuration that requires a sequence switch on or indeed if you have not explained how to get into the program.

ESTABLISH THE PROBLEMS OF THE TASK

No task is without its problems. If you have done the task for some while then you know what those problems and pitfalls are. Make a list of them, you will need to warn your delegatee.

DEFINE AND ESTABLISH AUTHORITY

Define any additional authority needed. Remember to check the authority level table and make sure that you give enough authority for the task to be completed.

Establish the authority with anyone who might withhold the delegatee's right to do a task. Remember this could include quite junior people who pay out expenses, for example, and can only work to the set of rules given to them.

EXPLAIN THE TASK

Begin by setting the task in context: why it has to be done, where it falls within the whole task of the team. Then explain its good points and the potential problems. Those who think they have hit a problem for the first time very rarely rationalize; they either cover it up or stop work. You would prefer them to be aware of the problem and take it in their stride.

Remember too to delegate the right to be wrong. If yours is a blame culture, people will see mistakes as something to deny but if your delegatee is to learn then he or she will have to learn from mistakes as well as successes.

GO THROUGH THE TASK

Don't just tell them, show them. This is obvious if you are teaching someone a mechanical or manual task but not so obvious for a clerical or brain-type task. But it is a lot easier to remember how to do something if you can picture it being done properly in the first place.

The best way to do this is to show them the task as you do it at normal speed. Then slow down and do it again, this time talking them through every step you take, even the very minor ones.

WATCH THE DELEGATEE GO THROUGH THE TASK

Stay put and let the delegatee have a go at the task under your eyes. Don't be quick to criticize if he or she does it wrong; people respond better if you just ask them if they are sure about that part of the task and give them a chance to think it through again.

ESTABLISH SUCCESS CRITERIA

Success in any task can be measured using the four key words:

- quality
- quantity
- time
- cost

For example, a task could be outlined as follows:

> Fifty invoices processed with an error rate no higher than one per cent within three days using the resources available.

> By 4 March (time) you should have written the outline of the report (quantity) so that it is ready for final checking (quality). You can use my secretary to help with the typing if necessary (cost).

SET REPORT-BACK TARGETS

Make it clear what should be done by what time and to what standard. Use the success criteria to make landmarks along the road to completion.

MONITOR

Don't just say 'my door is always open' – be there at an agreed time. If you want the task done by 5.00pm on Friday ask for completion by 10.00am. If the task is perfect you have plenty of time; if it is 95 per cent correct you'll still be pleased because you have time to put if right without panicking; but if you ask for it to be completed by 5.00pm you may be angry when that task is only 95 per cent correct.

Monitoring does not mean breathing down someone's neck, hanging over them to see how they are doing. It simply means maintaining agreed checkpoints along the way.

And when they bring the task to you and say 'I'm stuck', ask them to list three things they could do next. If you ask for three there is a fair chance that one of them will be correct. Then ask the delegatee to choose which of the three possible solutions he or she would opt for. Try to guide your delegatee towards the best solutions but make sure that the decisions and learning curves are theirs.

Never, never say 'Oh leave it with me, I'll sort it out'. First that is very demoralizing and second, they'll only learn to upward-delegate whenever a task gets tricky. And upward delegation is a terrible waste of your time.

There are many tasks on which you can practise delegation. You can use real tasks but in Exercise 9.4 I have given you an interesting if commonplace task to try: one I use a great deal in my workshops with quite a few humorous results.

SUMMARY

Drop-in visitors are a big waste of time. Of course, some social conversation is essential: it helps to build a team and it rests the brain but don't fool yourself that all conversations are worthwhile – some are not. If you can move the office around it usually makes a big difference, but if you can't then try the tricks in this chapter: they will help. If nothing else they will make other departments curious and that might help them to control their use of your time and their drop-in habits.

Delegation is essential for a cost-effective organization that develops and grows. Don't be the weak link in the chain of cost-effective working.

Finally, to get the most from this chapter you now need to work through some, if not all, of the exercises that follow.

EXERCISES

Exercise 9.1 – You're sitting where?

The purpose of this exercise is to help team members maximize the use of their office space.
　　You will need:

- flipcharts
- large sheets of brown paper
- scissors, rulers, pencils, pens
- Post-it™ notes in various colours
- plenty of space to work on

Spread out the brown paper on a flat surface and cut it to scale to represent your office space. Mark the doors and windows, plug sockets that cannot be moved, etc. with felt-tip pen.
　　Now cut Post-it™ notes to shape and scale to represent the desks, filing cabinets, photocopiers and other kit in your office.
　　Let everyone take part in replanning the office. If a plan looks like it might work, copy it onto a flipchart sheet and carry on until you have at least three options that can be used singly or combined in some way.
　　Remember, you will have to check with office services or house management and possibly your boss before you make any major changes but even the very small ones might make a big difference, so don't be disheartened by the need for permission.

Exercise 9.2 – People tactics

The purpose of this exercise is to help the team devise its own list of tactics for preventing drop-in visitors.
　　You will need:

- flipcharts
- coloured flipchart pens
- Interruption log sheets compiled over at least a week.

Begin by asking everyone to compile an interruption log. Ask them to record every interruption, including all the good ones and any interruptions from you or your boss.

Next, ask everyone to categorize their interruption log findings into the following categories:

- essential interruptions to help me do my job
- interruptions from other departments (categorized by department)
- interruptions from subordinates
- interruptions from colleagues
- interruptions from bosses
- socializing interruptions
- telephone interruptions
- non-essential interruptions
- interruptions because I did not explain enough
- any other category that has more than two entries in it.

Change or expand the categories to suit your own needs; this list is only an example.

Working together and using the flipcharts, look for patterns in the interruptions experienced by the team. What could you do about them? Have the team brainstorm for solutions using the material in this chapter and any of the rest of this book you have already covered.

Exercise 9.3 – Delegation quiz

The purpose of this exercise is to make individuals aware of the need to delegate. First answer the questions yourself and then give the list to at least one team member to answer for you. Do the results tally?

You will need copies of the quiz in Figure 9.6. Then as a result of the quiz make a list of the tasks that could be delegated and write a delegation plan. For this part of the exercise you will need:

- flipcharts (one per three members of the team)
- coloured pens
- copies of the completed delegation quiz.

Do you need to delegate more?

1. Do you take work home more than once a month? ☐ Yes ☐ No
2. Do you work longer hours than those you supervise? ☐ Yes ☐ No
3. Are you frequently interrupted because others come to you with questions or for advice or decisions? ☐ Yes ☐ No
4. Do you spend some of your working time doing things for others which they could do for themselves? ☐ Yes ☐ No
5. Do you have unfinished jobs accumulating, difficulty meeting deadlines? ☐ Yes ☐ No
6. Do you spend more of your time working on details than planning and supervising? ☐ Yes ☐ No
7. Do you trust others to do the job as well as you might do it yourself? ☐ Yes ☐ No
8. Do you work at details because you enjoy them, although someone else could do them? ☐ Yes ☐ No
9. Do you doubt your staff's abilities to take on more responsibility? ☐ Yes ☐ No
10. Are you a perfectionist, too conscientious about details that are not important for the main objectives of the job in hand? ☐ Yes ☐ No
11. Do you keep job details secret from staff? ☐ Yes ☐ No
12. Do you believe that you do your best work under pressure? ☐ Yes ☐ No
13. Would you hesitate to admit that you need help to remain on top of your job? ☐ Yes ☐ No
14. Do you fail to ask the team for their ideas about problems that arise at work? ☐ Yes ☐ No
15. Do you believe it is quicker to do it yourself? ☐ Yes ☐ No

No one is perfect but with more than 6 yes replies you should delegate more. With more than 12 yes replies plan for your heart attack now – it won't be long in coming.

FIGURE 9.6: The delegation quiz

The Aftermath

As a team make a list of the tasks that could be delegated. Now divide them into three lists:

- easy-to-delegate tasks
- short-term or one-off tasks
- tricky but long-term tasks

How could these tasks be delegated? In whole or in part? Who could tackle the task? Who wants to?

Brainstorm the session and build your delegation plan.

Plan

Task to be delegated   **To whom**   **By when**

Exercise 9.4 – Tie me a knot

This exercise will help anyone learn to delegate. You don't have to use the task described here; however, since it is a simple one that most of your team (certainly the men) will know how to do and yet will find hard to explain, it is a good task to demonstrate the need for really effective delegation. Try the task before discussing the section earlier in this chapter on delegating effectively. Then use the full instructions to get someone else in the team to delegate it well.

You will need:

- flipchart
- coloured flipchart pens
- one tie per team member.

Ask one of the men in your team to explain to the rest of the team how to tie a Windsor knot in a tie. Give the individual no hints, just let him loose on the subject.

Tell those learning to follow the directions they receive and only those directions, no others. For example, if the delegator says 'put the tie round your neck' don't put it under a collar, just round the neck. Considering putting it round the neck so that the long ends hang at the back.

Once the team have tried to tie a Windsor knot go through the delegation techniques with them, pointing out how the tying of the tie can be delegated. We often have fun with setting the tie in context.

■ Why to men wear ties? To catch food that misses the mouth?
■ What use is the tie? To cover the missing shirt buttons?
■ What are the pitfalls? Knots that miss the collar? A short fat end and long thin end?

How to Tie a Windsor Knot

1. Drape the tie round the neck, under the collar. The wide part of the tie should be on the left-hand side and twice the length of the narrower part which is hanging on the right-hand side of the neck.
2. Hold the short, narrower end of the tie in your right hand all the time you are tying the tie; do *not* release it.
3. Cross the left-hand side of the tie in front of the right, making a circle round the neck. Now pass the left-hand side up through the circle and over to the right-hand side.
4. Pass the left-hand side of the tie behind the knot being formed and up through the centre and over the left-hand side of the knot.
5. With the longest part of the tie in your left hand pass it over the total knot being formed and up through the centre. The long part of the tie is now in the middle of the circle, parallel with your nose.
6. Finally, pass the widest and longest part of the tie through the front piece to complete the knot. You now have a wide loose knot.
7. To form a tighter, tidy knot pull the front (wider) part of the tie.
8. To adjust the tie to your neck measurement and fit neatly under the collar, pull the back thin piece of the tie.

READING LIST

Although this section is called a reading list the best extra
information is in the form of videos and CD-Rom. They are
reviewed below.

The Unorganised Manager Parts 1 & 2 (Video Arts)
Getting rather long in the tooth now and somewhat sexist for today's
audience, it remains a good overview of time management
techniques. A dramatized story with humour. *Score: 6*

The Unorganised Sales Manager Parts 1 & 2 (Video Arts)
An updated version of the above, designed specifically for sales teams.
A dramatized story with humour. *Score: 8*

The Paper Chase (Video Arts)
Based on the book by Declan Tracey, a dramatized video with
humour that concentrates on clearing your desk and filing paper.
The long-winded introduction by Anthony Jay should be omitted
when you use it. *Score: 9*

Positive Time Skills (Fenman)
A factual checklist of tips. By no means funny but invaluable for the
commonsense approach it advocates. *Score: 8*

Managing Time (BBC)
A documentary-style programme in two parts looking at time
management and the individual in Part 1 and time management and
others in Part 2. *Score: 7*

Time to Think (Training Direct)
A dramatized video that covers all the key points. It offers eight golden rules of time management. *Score: 8*

30 Ways to Make More Time (Melrose)
An excellent dramatized video backed by John Adair and based on his book *How to Manage your Time*. *Score: 9*

The Time Trap 11 (Melrose)
An American dramatized video that covers all the points if you can take the American style. *Score: 7*

Making your Time Count (Training Direct CD-Rom)
All the advantages of interactive training and bang up to date. *Score: 1*

A Matter of Time (Training Direct CD-Rom)
Another time management CD that is bang up to date. *Score: 7*

The above suggestions are available from:

BBC
BBC for Business
PO Box 77, Wetherby
West Yorkshire
LS23 7HN
Tel: 01937 840 222
Fax: 01937 845 381

Training Direct
Longman House
Burnt Mill
Harlow
Essex CM20 2JE
Tel: 01279 623 927
Fax: 01279 623 739

Fenman
Fenman Training
Clive House
The Business Park
Ely
Cambs CB7 4EH
Tel: 01353 665 533
Fax: 01353 663 644

Video Arts Ltd
Dumbarton House
68 Oxford Street
London
W1N 0LH
Tel: 0171 637 7288
Fax: 0171 580 8103

Melrose
Melrose Learning Resources
16 Bromells Road
London
SW4 0BL
Tel: 0171 627 8404
Fax: 0171 622 0421

BOOKS

There are so many books in print on time management that it is impossible to list even a few. If you want to read a book go to a good business bookshop and find one that has a style matching your own, with messages that reinforce rather than start all over again.

INDEX

Action pile, 93–94, 99
Agenda, 127
  items, 124–126
  setting exercise, 133
  writing exercise, 132
Attitude, 20, 24
Attitude survey:
  exercise, 24

Body language, 73
Building new habit paths:
  exercise, 25

Cards:
  dragon, 81
  fear, 80
Change, 21, 22, 34–35
change plan, 21–22
Clear desk policy, 65, 89–92, 102
  exercise, 102–103
Clutter:
  exercise, 103–104
Communication, 15, 106
  faxes, 107, 115
  letters, 107–109, 111
  letters and faxes exercise, 119
  listening, 116–118
  memos, 107
  telephone, 106, 113–116
Contemplative tasks, 31
Constructive tasks, 31
Crises, 5, 11, 37, 47
Crisis management, 11, 47

Decision-making chart, 130
Delegation, 16, 33, 64, 141, 150
  authority, 151–152
  exercise, 158–159
  how to do it, 152–153
  monitor, 154
  power, 150, 152

quiz, 156–158
Destructive tasks, 31
Diaries, 44
  control, 48
  sheets, 45–47
  simple rules, 44–45
Dragon cards, 81

Elephant files, 94, 99
Exercises:
  attitude survey, 24
  building new habit paths, 25
  clear that desk, 102–103
  clutter swamp, 103–104
  delegation quiz, 156–158
  habit track, 25
  here be the dragons, 79–81
  I'm sorry I can't do that, 81–82
  just get off the line, 120
  letters and faxes, 119
  people tactics, 155–156
  prioritize the in-tray, 51–53
  procrastination party, 78
  setting an agenda, 133
  taking control, 53–55
  team diary match, 56
  team roles, 138–139
  team rules, 139–140
  tie me a knot, 158–159
  time – where does it go?, 2–12
  what did we just agree?, 133
  write an agenda, 132
  write a mission statement, 51
  you're sitting where?, 155

Fear, of, 66
  failure, 66, 69
  known, 66–68
  people, 66–67, 70
  unknown, 66, 68–69
Fear cards, 80

Faxes, 107, 115
  exercise, 119
Fog testing, 102, 112, 119
Files:
  dead, 101
  active, 100
  categories of, 101
  colour-coded, 101
  elephant, 94, 99
Filing system, 89, 98, 100–101
  cabinets, 99, 100, 102

Habits, 13, 19–20, 24
  building new habit paths:
    exercise, 25
  change plan, 21–22
  habit track:
    exercise, 25
  paths, 20, 22
  tasks, 31
Here be the dragons:
  exercise, 79–81

I'm sorry I can't do that:
  exercise, 81–82
Importance and urgency, 40–41
Important tasks, 31, 40
Instruct-a-task, 31
Interruptions, 16, 141–142, 147–149
  drop in visitors, 145, 146
  office layout, 142, 143–146, 149
  people tactics:
    exercise, 155–156
  telephone, 145

Just get off the line:
  exercise, 120

Key:
  organization time, 47
  personal time, 46

Letters, 107
  fog testing, 112
  layout, 108–109
  punctuation, 108, 111
  sentences, 108, 110–111
  vocabulary, 108–111
  exercise, 119
Life pattern sheets, 47

Manage your mind, 22–23
Management Learning Resources Limited,
    138
Meetings, 15, 46, 121
  agendas, 121–127
  any other business, 126
  exercises, 132–133
  decision-making chart, 129–131
  flipcharts, 126, 129, 131–132
  matters arising, 126
  minutes:
    exercise, 133–138
  note-takers, 122

note-taking, 126
  rules, 127, 129
  seating plan, 128–129, 131
  team roles:
    exercise, 138–139
  team rules:
    exercise, 139–140
Memos, 107
Mission statements, 14, 36–37
  characteristics, 37
  key elements, 39
  questions, 37–38
  writing exercise, 51
Objectives, 14
  personal, 44

Office layout, 142, 144–146
  office space:
    exercise, 155
  open plan, 142–143
  shared, 142
  solo, 142, 145–146

Panic tasks, 31
Paper, 15, 88, 102
  clear desk policy, 89–92
  clear the briefcase, 98–99
  filing, 102–103
Paperwork piles:
  action, 93–94, 102–103
  information, 95, 99, 102–103
  reading, 95, 102–103
  rubbish, 96–97, 99, 102–103
People tactics:
  exercise, 155–156
Personal diary:
  rules, 44–45
Priorities, 14, 28
Prioritize the in-tray:
  exercise, 51–53
  answers, 56–58
Prioritizing, 36, 39, 42–44, 48
  rules, 48
Procrastination, 14, 59–60, 64, 77
  consequences of, 63
  exercise, 78
  fear, conquering it, 65–70
  items, analysis of, 61–62
  procrastinated tasks, 64–65

Quality, 89
Questionnaire:
  time – where does it go?, 2–12
Quiet hour concept, 113–116
Quiz:
  delegation, 156–158

Reactive tasks, 31
Real tasks, 31
Role plays, 81, 120

Saying no –
  constructively, 71–72
  exercises, 81–87

Saying no – (*cont.*)
  generally, 76–77
  saying no to:
    colleagues, 74–75, 85
    dumpers, 76, 87
    other departments, 75–76
    your boss, 72–73
    your boss's boss, 73–74, 84
Setting an agenda:
  exercise, 133
Solo tasks, 31

Taking control:
  exercise, 53–55
Tasks, 31
  analysis of, 40
  importance and urgency of, 40–41, 48
  progressive, 41–43, 48
  styles of, 32–33
  support, 41, 43, 48
Team:
  exercises, 56, 138–140
  members, 34–35
  patterns, 34
  roles, 128–129, 138–139
  rules, 50, 139–140
  tasks, 31
Telephone:
  exercise, 120
  interruptions, 145
  listening, 116–118
Time:
  improvement, 34
  where does it go?:
    questionnaire, 2–12
    why audit it? 27–28

Time audit, 13, 27
  general terms analysis, 30
  questions, 29
  rationale, 32
  sheets, 29
  work time analysis, 31
Training, 38
  sessions, 49
  team contract, 49–50
Transactional analysis (TA), 18, 23

Urgent tasks, 31
Urgency and prioritizing, 40, 42–43

Values, 55
Vital documents, 89
Vocabulary, 108, 109, 110

What did we just agree?:
  exercise, 133
Write:
  an agenda, 132
  a mission statement, 51
Writing, 107
  faxes, 107, 115
  fog testing, 112
  layout, 108–109
  letters, 107
  memos, 107
  punctuation, 108, 111
  readability, 112
  sentences, 108, 109, 110
  vocabulary, 108, 109, 110

You're sitting where?:
  exercise, 155